The Man with the Turquoise Eyes

The Man with the Turquoise Eyes

And Other True Stories of a Private Eye's Search for Missing Persons

Norma Mott Tillman, Private Investigator
with
David Hunter

Rutledge Hill Press

Nashville, Tennessee

Published by Rutledge Hill Press, Inc.
211 Seventh Avenue North
Nashville, Tennessee 37219

Distributed in Canada by H. B. Fenn & Company, Ltd., 1090 Lorimar Drive, Mississauga, Ontario, L5S 1R7

Typography by D&T/Bailey Typesetting, Inc., Nashville, Tennessee.

Library of Congress Cataloging-in-Publication Data

Tillman, Norma Mott, 1938–
    The man with the turquoise eyes : and other true stories of a private eye's search for missing persons / Norma Mott Tillman with David Hunter.
        p. cm.
    ISBN 1-55853-359-1 (hardcover)
    1. Missing persons—United States—Investigation—Case studies.
2. Tracking and trailing—United States—Case studies.   I. Hunter, David. 1947– .   II. Title.
HV6762.U5T57   1995
362.8—dc20   95-38487
                                                          CIP

Printed in the United States of America
95 96 97 98 99 — 8 7 6 5 4 3 2 1

To my wonderful family, thank you again for understanding why I can't find enough time to do all the things I want to do. I don't mean to neglect any of you—you are my reason for existing and I love you more than you'll ever know.

And to all the searchers who need to find a missing relative or friend. I understand the need to fill a void in your heart, to have closure with the past, to put an end to the unknown, and to be able to go on with your life. I hope you all find and are reunited with your missing loved ones. I want to encourage each of you to complete your search because I know that whatever you discover, you can live with it. It's the unknown that hurts so much. I sincerely believe that the truth will set you free.

Contents

Acknowledgments

WHEN I MENTIONED to my publisher, Larry Stone, that I would like to write a book about some of the people I have located and reunited, it never occurred to me that Larry would want another book so soon after *How to Find Almost Anyone, Anywhere* was released.

Needless to say, I was thrilled that he would consider another book right away. Almost immediately, mixed emotions took over. Of course I was anxious to do it, but how in the world could I possibly find the time to concentrate? I had too much going on—I just signed a contract for a possible television show and I was already so far behind in my work that I did not even have time to answer the phone, much less work the active cases that were beginning to back up. Hundreds of people write me each week, and hundreds more call. I began to feel totally out of control because I had more to do than I could possibly handle in twenty-four hours. I was feeling stress from not being able to handle my busy schedule and workload. Each person who called wanted me to do something—immediately. I think I know how the person at McDonald's who takes drive-thru orders must feel. Everyone just calls and places their order like I don't have anything else in the world to do but wait on them.

I told Larry how busy I was and that I really wanted to do the book, but I didn't think I could do it immediately. What a shock and surprise it was when Larry suggested that I meet David Hunter, a writer with whom Larry had already published seven mystery books. I had seen David's books when I visited Rutledge Hill, and I knew that he was an experienced law-enforcement officer, but why did Larry want me to meet David? The next thing I knew Larry invited me to join him and David for lunch.

Knowing that Larry has been in the publishing business for a long time and has a very good track record, I completely trust and respect his judgment. Little did I expect what was about to happen.

During lunch, Larry suggested that David and I become partners on this book, for me to furnish my cases and experiences and for David to do the writing. My first reaction was that I am too independent to work with a partner. I like it this way. I choose to do everything alone—I don't want or need a partner to get in my way.

David and I did what all detectives do when they get together, we swapped "war stories." Of course with our backgrounds, we had a lot in common, but David was not a private investigator and private investigation is a different ballgame from law enforcement. As a private investigator you have to be totally independent, with no one to back you up, no dispatcher to ask for directions or assistance, no superior to tell you what to do or not to do. I didn't ask, but I imagine David had much the same reaction. Why did he need to work with me? He had enough material from his own experiences. Surely he didn't need a partner either.

After lunch, I invited David back to my office for a few demonstrations of my computer databases. I explained to him that as a private investigator I had access to more information than I did when I worked in law enforcement, but I don't think he believed me until I showed him what I could do. As we became acquainted, we each agreed that we thought Larry's vision about this project was probably a good idea and that it was a win-win situation. I didn't have time to write and David did. David seemed willing to take on the challenge of writing someone else's experiences. After all the challenge is what makes both law enforcement officers and private investigators enjoy their job.

The bigger the challenge, the bigger the thrill. It's the satisfaction of doing something that is not easy, routine, dull, or boring. *Challenge* is the real reason I enjoy being a private eye and what makes each search interesting, exciting, and satisfying. *Challenge* is the reason I worked in law enforcement and the reason I had to learn to fly an airplane. I just had to see if I could do it. To me, finding a missing loved one is the *ultimate challenge*—even better than finding one of the ten most wanted! It is totally awesome to realize that reuniting loved ones makes such a difference in their lives—it mends a broken heart, it heals the void and pain of living with the unknown, it cures psychological problems that arise as a result of having a need to find someone and not being able to do so.

The more I thought about David doing the writing, the more I became convinced that working with a partner might not be such a bad idea. It would be different, but as I always say, "nothing ventured, nothing gained." After a lot of thought, I called Larry and told him that I thought working with David on this book would be fine with me. It turned out to be one of the best decisions I could have made.

David was very patient and understanding. He absorbed every word I said as I described the cases and how I worked them. David had a very difficult task before him, for he had to write the book as if he were me. That meant that David had to think like me and react like me. He and I do not always think alike. For some reason, David assumed I cry a lot. In fact, he had me shedding tears on every case—which rarely happens! If I do cry, they are tears of joy, for being so happy that I have helped another person. Other than that, I think David's final edition of this book is a masterpiece. When I read it the first time I thought "what a great writer he is, like an artist painting a beautiful picture on a canvas." I could hardly believe my cases and experiences could be portrayed so eloquently. It was at this point that I realized, understood, and appreciated why Larry teamed us up. I am grateful to both of them.

Of course, Larry also had the vision to team David and me with two wonderful editors, Anne Christian Buchanan and Amy Lyles Wilson, who both seem to have a special talent for taking over and adding the "icing to the cake."

Thanks team. Each of you is terrific and I'm glad I had the opportunity to work with you. I am delighted with the finished product and hope that this book becomes a best-seller.

The Man with the
Turquoise Eyes

1

Everybody Wants to Find Somebody

THE INQUIRIES come in by the hundreds now to the office of my small Nashville detective agency. A part-time employee spends each day sorting the letters and filing them in manila folders representing distinct categories: "Children Looking for Parents," "Parents Looking for Children," "People Looking for Lost Loves." The phone rings almost constantly these days. My fax machine spits out paper by the hour.

And almost every letter, each phone call, each fax is a variation of the same request—the same yearning, the same hope. One person has lost track of another person. Somebody wants to find somebody else.

And that's what I do. I find people who have been lost and reunite people who have been separated. And through my work I have become one of the most widely known private investigators in recent history, at least in my specialized field. Literally millions of people have watched me on national television as I explained my investigative skills and presided over on-the-air reunions.

This explosion of success has surprised me as much as anyone else. When I first decided to go into this line of work, I was afraid there might not be enough business to pay my rent. But now I know that I need not have worried—because everybody has somebody he or she wants to find. Literally everyone I meet is a potential client.

I decided to prove this point one day while having lunch with some colleagues. I asked the waitress who was putting our salads on the table whether there was someone she would like to find. She hesitated only a moment. Then she began to tell us about an old friend she had lost contact with years ago.

It's like that wherever I go. At parties, people often approach me the same way they approach doctors about medical problems. (And like a doctor, I have learned to tell them to call me during office hours. Otherwise, I would have no private life.) Even at conventions where I am addressing other private investigators, my colleagues will often come by and tell me discreetly that they too have a personal need for my specialized services. I guess they realize that just as surgeons shouldn't operate on family members, investigators should turn emotionally charged issues over to other professionals.

Once, during a conference of investigators, a colleague and I were talking about missing person cases as we stood in front of a restroom mirror, combing our hair and repairing our makeup. We were preparing to leave when a voice called out from one of the stalls: "Wait!" Moments later, a somewhat flustered woman emerged.

"I'm sorry," she told us, blushing slightly. "I didn't mean to eavesdrop, but I heard you talking about finding missing persons. I have an old acquaintance I'd really like to locate. I've never been able to work up the courage to call a private detective, so when I heard the two of you talking, I decided it was now or never."

She dropped her eyes for a moment, still uncomfortable, then looked back at us again. "Could you help me?"

"Of course," I told her, handing her one of my cards. A few weeks later, she was reunited with an old flame, and I had the warm satisfaction of having helped her bring closure to an unresolved area of her life.

That kind of challenge is the reason I stay in this business. No matter how many letters and calls and faxes come in, I am always keenly aware that each case stored in my overflowing metal filing cabinets represents a living, breathing human being—someone I might be able to help.

I am well aware, of course, that the person who wrote the letter or made the call will not be the only one touched if an investigation is successful. You cannot launch such a search without making waves. That means an investigator like me holds an awesome responsibility. But it is a responsibility that I gladly accept. To me there is no greater reward, no more joyous event, than the successful reunion of two people who have been separated by time and circumstances.

How can you set a price on the expression of a young woman who is seeing her mother for the first time? How can you determine the cost of a grandmother's joy when she holds a grandchild she didn't know existed, or calculate the wonder of lost loves finding each other after years spent apart? Those are the kinds of rewards that keep me in the people-finding business. Of course I need the money to stay in operation. But I really enjoy the happy endings.

That's not to say that *every* case of mine has a storybook conclusion. There are times when a "lost" person doesn't want to be found, when reunited people don't get along, or when I simply cannot solve a case. And there are times when I struggle with moral dilemmas: Does the desire for privacy on the part of a newly found person outweigh the hopes and dreams of the client who has hired me to find that person? Am I really helping a client by presenting him or her with painful information? Is a talk-show reunion worth exposing a client to public scrutiny at an emotionally vulnerable time?

There is no manual, no set of commandments to cover all possible situations in my line of work. Some cases require the wisdom of Solomon and the patience of Job. And yet my experience has been that the vast majority of my lost-and-found cases *do* have happy endings—and that there is a lot I can do to make such conclusions even more likely.

I have found, for instance, that even people who react negatively to being confronted with the past will almost always come around eventually if they are treated with patience, understanding, and tact. I have also learned that for almost all clients, bad news is infinitely preferable to no news at all. Even those few clients who learn bad news about their pasts usually express relief and a sense of freedom that at least now they *know*.

As I said, I like to see happy endings. But it has not been easy achieving national recognition and respect in a profession that has sometimes been noted for its sleazy operators. Too often, the movie image of an unshaven, slovenly man in a dirty trench coat, peeping through bedroom windows and staring at life through the bottom of a shot glass, is the one that springs to mind when the subject of private detectives comes up. And unfortunately, that image has sometimes been accurate, especially in the past and in states where professional requirements were minimal. That's certainly not the way professional investigators operate today. Most of us are regulated by law and must meet minimum requirements of education and experience even to qualify for a license.

Sometimes, as you will read in this book, happy endings require a lot of work and preparation on my part. Occasionally, in fact, my continuing efforts to bring people together go on longer than is profitable—if you count profit in terms of dollars and cents. But to me it is worth it, especially in those cases that appeared hopeless at first, when I am rewarded with tears of joy and hugs between family members being reunited after many years of being apart.

As for public recognition, I have been in the spotlight enough to satisfy anyone. How many people are lucky enough to be written up in such national magazines as *Cosmopolitan*, *Good Housekeeping*, and *Family Circle* just for doing a job they enjoy? And how many have the opportunity to be interviewed before an audience of millions by the likes of Oprah Winfrey, Sally Jessy Raphael, Vicki Lawrence, Leeza Gibbons, and Geraldo Rivera?

But my forays into television and magazine fame have not been undertaken for the purpose of basking in the limelight. The publicity is just another means to reach more people with my services. I believe that fame when pursued for its own sake is an empty vessel. The real satisfaction is in a job well done, in providing hope for those who have given up, and in giving comfort to those battered by a seemingly cold and uncaring world.

Every new investigation is a journey into the unknown, an expedition into uncharted waters complete with killer winds and jagged reefs. It is my task to help my clients and their loved ones negotiate the difficult channels and steer them through the storms. It is a job I relish, a task for which I sometimes feel that Divine Providence has prepared me. My background seems to have led me straight to my present occupation, uniquely qualified.

I never actually said, "I want to be a private investigator when I grow up." But when other little girls were playing with dolls, I could often be found reading my police detective father's graphic manuals on homicide investigation, absorbing such terms as *decapitation*, *rape*, and *homicide*. Such reading material wasn't, mind you, something my parents encouraged. Like my father's revolver, the police books were not left for me to find. After all, it was understood back then that little boys grew up to become policemen and firemen, and little girls grew up to be housewives and schoolteachers.

Everyone understood it except me. From an early age, I had my own distinct ideas about what was appropriate for my life. If my father, the police detective, who had trained as a mechanical engineer, could break out of what he considered a monotonous life and embark on an adventurous career, I saw no reason why things should be different for me.

Even as a very young child, I always thrived on challenge, both physical and mental. My earliest library books were mysteries, and I usually solved them long before I finished reading. And I loved the outdoors; among my happiest memories are the summers I spent at camp, sleeping in tents, building trails, cooking over open fires, and learning to fend for myself. When I grew too old to go to camp, I became a counselor.

And all that time, I dreamed of a life that would really count for something. I longed for a career that was truly "MADE in the USA"—*mystery*, *adventure*, *danger*, and *excitement*.

The first real hint my parents had that I did not intend to fit into anyone's mold may have been my decision to move to Washington, DC, soon after graduating from Nashville's East High School, instead of enrolling in a local college or announcing my engagement, as so many of my classmates had done. I made the move on the spur of the moment, landed a job in the Department of Commerce by sheer good fortune, and spent a wonderful year on my own enjoying the giddy freedom of being young and free in a fascinating city.

I would probably still be living in Washington if my mother had not fallen ill suddenly and died. But she did, and I had a father and two younger sisters who needed me. I moved back home, took a job with the Internal Revenue Service, and started night school, where I met my future husband. Sonny thought he was marrying June Cleaver. Was he in for a surprise!

Not that I planned it this way. I tried to be a good housewife. I just got bored easily and needed challenges in my life. The care of three daughters proved a sufficient challenge for several years. They were my first priority, and I loved being home as long as they were there. But as soon as the youngest started school, I decided that it was time for me to find something to do during those now-free hours—preferably something exciting.

I got my first taste of law enforcement as a small-town police dispatcher, and I was infected almost immediately with what cops call "blue light fever." From there I moved to the world of big-city cops. My class picture from the police academy is on the wall of my office. It pretty well bears out the idea—then still very much in vogue—that police work was men's work. Of the forty new graduates in the picture, only five of us are women.

"I don't know who let *you* in," the training officer said, leaning down in my face that first day, "but I'll see that you don't make it through."

That prophecy very nearly came true when my foot caught in an automobile tire as my squad was running an obstacle course. I knew the ankle was broken as soon as my foot touched the ground again, but the training officer who had predicted that I would never make it immediately began to scream for me to get up and run. I was determined that he was not going to break me.

"Grab my hand!" the recruit ahead of me said, reaching back. With his help, I managed to run another quarter of a mile before finally collapsing in agony. I hadn't finished the run, and I had disobeyed a direct order. I was certain I would never graduate.

The next morning, however, when the training officer realized that I had run on a broken ankle, his attitude suddenly changed. I don't know whether this was because he saw I was determined or because he feared the consequences of his mistreating a recruit. To me, it didn't matter why. I was excused from physical training for the duration of training, and I finished the police academy near the top of my class.

For several years after graduating I was immersed in the police culture, busy acquiring firearm proficiency, an understanding of criminal law, accident investigation and hostage negotiation skills, self-defense, emergency medical training, and many other law enforcement necessities. I soon found, however, that I was not satisfied as a player on someone else's team. I wanted to run the show.

My next move was away from the police department to become an insurance fraud investigator. After acquiring a private investigator's license, I struck out to form my own agency, Unlimited Facts Obtained (UFO), Inc., in 1987.

At last I was my own boss, doing an exciting job that fulfilled my private childhood dream of challenge and adventure. The rest of the story, for those who have read my recent book, *How to Find Almost Anyone, Anywhere*, is history.

In that book, which has become a manual for both amateur and professional investigators across America, I taught many enthusiastic readers the basic techniques of how to conduct a search. But a funny thing happened on the way to the bestseller list.

The brief and often sketchy glimpses of the people cited as examples in my how-to book caused an almost immediate outcry from readers: They wanted a more personal, in-depth look at the people and events found in *How to Find Almost Anyone, Anywhere*. The book you are now reading will, I hope, satisfy that curiosity.

This, then, is a book of true adventures. Each one tells the story of living, breathing human beings. If I have done my job well, however, those specific human beings will not be easy to recognize—even to those who know them well. Privacy and protection are relevant issues in any work of nonfiction, and when you consider the nature of my business as a private investigator, the stakes are raised. How do I tell a true story about what I do without exposing people—many of them former clients—and without violating a trust I consider no less binding than that between doctors or lawyers and their clients?

What I have done—as many a writer of true stories has done—is to disguise the stories by using a number of literary devices or techniques. The first of these is familiar to anyone who has ever watched the old *Dragnet* television shows. Each episode featured a disclaimer: "The names have been changed to protect the innocent." In this book I have changed the names of *all* the people I write about—guilty or innocent. Dates, periods of time, ages, circumstances, and geographic locations have also been disguised. And I have used a device known to writers as time compression. That simply means that a story that transpired over a period of six months may be reduced to a period of days to keep things from dragging. Everything in such a story is true, but the timeframe is shortened for the sake of readability—and to make it harder to recognize.

It goes without saying, then, that any use of a real name in this book is strictly coincidental. All possible means of protecting individual privacy have been employed, and any inadvertent embarrassment I may have possibly caused to anyone is totally without malice.

The end product of my labors is an exciting look at cases that have come to me through the years, cases that live in my memories and that I hope will be memorable to you as well.

Enjoy.

2

Like a New Man Now

I PULLED INTO the long, tree-lined driveway, impressed by the well-manicured lawn. It was not what I expected from the saddest man I had ever met.

Allen Sprague was an expert on computers, both hardware and software. I had met him at a bank while I was working on a case. At the time, he was preparing to bring an entire new computer system on-line for the bank.

On one of his trips through the office where I was going over files, Allen had reluctantly stopped long enough to show me the restroom and to answer a couple of my questions about computers. As we talked, I was reminded of Eeyore from the Winnie the Pooh storybooks and cartoons.

You remember Eeyore, don't you? His face was perpetually sad. He spoke in a painfully slow and monotone voice to his friends Pooh, Piglet, and Tigger, saying things like, "That is how friends are sometimes. Here today and gone tomorrow."

In addition to his dragging, emotionless Eeyore voice, Allen had very deep-set eye sockets. Although he was actually quite handsome, his whole face seemed to droop. And he acted as if speaking to another human being was something he did only because it couldn't be avoided. The pain in his eyes was hard to look at.

Despite Allen's obvious desire to be left alone, I had persisted because at the time, in those early days of my career as a private detective, I had yet to acquire a much-needed computer. In the very beginning, I had viewed such devices as luxury items to be bought at a more prosperous time. But now I was beginning to think it was time to join the information age.

Allen had finally given me his card, more to get away from me, I think, than anything else. He told me to call him when I was ready to make a purchase and that he worked out of his house. He claimed never to have had an office nor done a minute's worth of advertising. He seemed proud that word of mouth kept him as busy as he wanted to be. His time was *very, very* expensive, he told me. I was a little surprised that he actually took the time to sit down and advise me. With Allen, it was really hard to tell whether he liked you. He never smiled or acted glad to see anybody.

Almost a year later, I found myself pulling up Allen's driveway, finally ready to get down to some serious computer business. A few of my customers who had actually paid their bills in full (and on time!) had given me enough spare cash to consider purchasing a used computer.

I had halfway expected Allen's home to look like the house where Norman Bates and his mother lived in Alfred Hitchcock's movie *Psycho*. Instead he lived in a cheerful, bright two-story structure, painted white and trimmed in pale yellow. Flowers were everywhere in abundance.

I was nervous as I rang the bell, even though he had invited me over. A moment later Allen answered the door. His basset-hound expression was in place as usual. I would later discover that he was in his early forties, but he looked much older. His beard was almost all silver, even though his hair was still dark.

"Come in," he said in his Eeyore voice. "Have a seat in my office. It's the first door on the left. I was just making some iced tea. Could I offer you a glass?"

"Please," I replied. I went down the short hallway, taking note of the Oriental rug under my feet, and took a seat beside the wooden table that apparently served as Allen's work table and desk. Staring around the room, I was fascinated by all the computer equipment—most of which was foreign to me.

A few minutes later he came in carrying a silver tray with two crystal glasses, silver iced-tea spoons, an ornate sugar bowl, and a small bowl of lemon slices. Each glass of tea was garnished with sprigs of mint. I was impressed.

"Exactly what will you be using your computer for?" Allen asked as he handed me my glass.

"Well . . . mostly for word processing and bills, I guess. And I've been reading about a couple of services I'd like to subscribe to—the kind where I can call up and get information over the phone."

"Oh, then you'll need a modem. . . ." By now he had sat down at his own computer and was typing in notes.

"I know you're a private investigator," he said. "Do you do anything besides bank work?"

"Yes," I answered. "I specialize in finding missing persons."

He looked directly at me, and there was more animation and interest in his eyes than I had ever seen before.

"What do you mean by *missing persons?*" he asked.

"Well, *missing persons* isn't exactly the right term, I guess. Most people aren't really missing; they just don't know that other people are looking for them."

"Suppose a son wanted to find his father, say after more than forty years. Would that be possible?"

"Probably," I replied. "It all depends on how much information you have to begin with."

Allen got up abruptly and left the room. For a moment I thought I had done something to offend him. Moments later, he was back. He handed me an eight-by-ten black-and-white photo (rather it was more of a sepia tone, the kind of photograph still in fashion during the Second World War).

I looked at the young soldier in the picture, then at Allen. They were obviously related. But there was a big difference. The man in the picture was smiling.

"Your father?" I asked.

"Yes," he said, sounding even more melancholy than usual. "The only thing I know about him is that his name was Keith Allen Mallory. I wouldn't know that if I hadn't seen it on my birth certificate."

"Your mother wouldn't give you any information?"

"No." I could hear a deep bitterness in his voice. "She took her secrets to the grave with her. She died hating my father. They got a divorce when I was less than a year old. She remarried and changed my name to her new married name.

"I was never allowed to discuss my father. The only thing she ever told me about him was that she had divorced him because he was running around with other women.

"After she died, though, I found this picture among her belongings. The way she treated me made more sense after I saw the picture. Apparently her hatred of my father extended to me because I look so much like him. She certainly didn't treat any-one else the way she treated me."

"It must have been hard for you," I said, somewhat lamely.

"Yes." He nodded and stared off into space with those basset-hound eyes. "Ever since my mother died, I've been looking in phonebooks everywhere I travel on business, hoping to find my father. It seems hopeless, though."

"No, it's not hopeless," I told him.

"Let's make a deal," he said, leaning in my direction and star-ing me directly in the eyes. "You find my father—or find out what you can about him and other people I might be related to, if he's no longer alive—and I'll build you a top-of-the-line computer with any kind of software you want."

"It's a deal," I said quickly.

Allen was a brilliant man. He already had the seed to his problem's solution, and what I was able to do, he could have done himself. But the hardest part of finding anyone is knowing how to begin.

After I left Allen's house that afternoon, I drove straight to the adjoining county where his parents had been living when they got their divorce. Armed with an approximate date, I quickly found the final divorce decree between Allen's mother and father. It had been there all along, less than fifty miles away, waiting for someone to open the dusty old files.

Unfortunately, the divorce decree didn't give me much additional information. Allen's father's full name and birthdate were listed, but no Social Security number was given. And Allen's mother had not asked for child support, so there had been no reason for the local court to maintain contact with his father. All I found was a general-delivery address in a small Missouri town, where the father had requested the final divorce decree be sent.

A good detective always looks for the most obvious solution to a problem, so I called directory assistance in the Missouri town. Unfortunately, there were no listings at all for anyone by the name of Mallory.

Next, I tried searching for a driver's license using the name and birthdate I had found in the divorce decree. No luck. I uncovered a fair number of Keith Allen Mallorys, and I called all who had a listed phone number, but none proved to be the man I needed. Possibly someone had entered the father's name incorrectly into the database, which does happen sometimes.

Finally, late one afternoon, I put down the receiver and took a deep breath. I was already planning a trip to West Tennessee. It wouldn't be that hard to squeeze in a side trip to Missouri.

The library in that little Missouri town was surprisingly well maintained, with up-to-date files and equipment. Obviously it was a place where the staff took great pride in their work. In less than thirty minutes I had ascertained through old phone books and city directories that nobody by the name of Mallory had been listed at a local address for at least ten years. A little disappointed, I asked the librarian for microfiche files of the local newspaper for the previous fifteen years, then settled in for a tedious search.

My diligence was quickly rewarded, however. I found an obituary for a Mrs. Tyler Mallory, who had died fourteen years earlier.

A Keith A. Mallory was listed as her son, as well as two daughters and several grandchildren.

Five minutes later, I had located one of the daughters in a current phone directory. She didn't answer when I dialed the number, but I decided to drive to her address. How far could it be?

I cruised slowly down the street, looking for the number I had written on the pad beside me. I spotted the house and pulled over to the curb. As I was climbing out of my rental car, an elderly woman in a very old but well-kept Ford pulled into the driveway. She got out of the car slowly, then walked toward the house, searching through her purse.

"Excuse me," I said quietly , so as not to startle her.

"Yes?" She leaned her head back to peer through her bifocals at me.

"Are you Mrs. Molly Swaney?"

"Yes, I am." Her eyes narrowed.

"And do you have a brother by the name of Keith Allen Mallory?"

"Yes. Is there something wrong with Keith?" Her voice was trembling, so I moved quickly to ease her fears. The question she had asked me was evidence that Allen's father was still alive and well.

"Not that I know of. I've been hired by a Mr. Allen Sprague to locate his father. I have reason to believe your brother may be the person I'm looking for."

"Allen Sprague?" For a moment, disappointment welled up in me. Had I come such a long way for nothing? Then her eyes lit up. "Oh, you mean *little Allen*. Yes, my brother had a son named Allen, but his ex-wife cut all ties with us forty years ago. My mother died grieving because she hadn't seen her grandchild since he was a baby."

"Well, Allen is alive and well and very much wants to meet his family," I told her.

Inside the house, Allen's aunt became more animated with every passing moment.

"Does Allen have any children? Does he look like Keith? Where does he live now?"

"May I use your phone, Mrs. Swaney?" I laughed aloud, happy that things were turning out well. "I think you need to speak to your nephew directly."

"Help yourself," she said. "I'll fix us something to drink."

A couple of minutes later, I waited as the phone rang at Allen's house, watching his aunt bustle around the quaint little kitchen. She reminded me of Aunt Bee on *The Andy Griffith Show*.

"Hello," Allen answered in that dead monotone of his.

"Allen, this is Norma Tillman. I'm here with your Aunt Molly. She would like to speak with you."

"I don't have an Aunt Molly," he said. "My mother only had one sister, and she's dead."

"But your *father* had two sisters."

"You've found my father?" It was the first real excitement I had ever heard in his voice.

"Not yet, but I'm at your Aunt Molly's house. She's going to talk to you and put you in contact with him. Are you ready?"

I could actually hear him swallow before he answered. "Yes. Yes, I am."

I handed the phone to Molly Swaney. "Hello, nephew," she said, her eyes suddenly filled with tears. "Have I got a lot of questions for you, young man."

An hour later, after finishing my third glass of lemonade, I put my card down on the kitchen table and quietly let myself out. Allen and his Aunt Molly were so deeply engrossed in talking about family matters that she didn't even notice when I left.

≈ ≈ ≈

"Delivery for Norma Tillman," the man at my office door said. I had to look at him closely before I realized that it was Allen Sprague. He appeared to have put on several pounds, and his eyes stood out as startling blue, no longer appearing sunken into the sockets. Most startling of all, though, he was smiling.

"You thought I'd forgotten, didn't you?" He pushed by me with a handcart on which he had stacked the components of a computer system.

"No, it hasn't been that long."

"It's been three weeks and four days," he said. "Do you want this computer on your desk?" Even his voice had changed, the Eeyore drag replaced by an animated baritone.

I stepped back and nodded, still a little shaken by the changes in Allen.

"You won't believe what's been happening in my life," he said, unpacking cardboard boxes. "I've met my father and a half-brother and half-sister and about a dozen cousins. For the first time in my life, I feel like I have roots. I feel like I *belong*. And I owe it all to you."

"It wasn't all that big a job," I told him, a little embarrassed.

"It was to me. When I get through, you're going to have a state-of-the-art computer to work with it. If it's been invented, it's in this computer. I've packed it with enough software to keep you busy for a year, just browsing through it."

"This is too much," I told him. "I know what a computer like this costs. The hours I put in, even with expenses, wouldn't have been a third of what this computer is worth."

"A deal's a deal," he said with a grin. "There's not enough money in the world to pay you back for what *I've* gotten out of it. You just don't know how I felt for years, day in and day out. I had no idea what it was like to be happy—not before you found my family!"

I swallowed a lump in my throat. *How many professions are there*, I thought to myself, *where you can touch human lives the way Allen has been touched*? He had literally become a new man— almost before my very eyes.

The computer was to be of more use to me than I had ever imagined. If I'd had it and the databases I now have when I first took Allen's case, I would have probably been able to find his father's Social Security number right away and located him much faster.

But I didn't know that back then. I did the best I could with what I had. And I got a new computer out of the deal. But it was secondary to the pleasure I received from seeing Allen transformed into a new—and happy—man.

3

Curiosity—
A Tool of the Trade

Do YOU EVER read any of the popular tabloids? You know, the ones with headlines like LOCH NESS MONSTER CAPTURED ALIVE, PRESIDENT'S WIFE HAS ALIEN CHILD, or ELVIS SPOTTED OUTSIDE GRACELAND!

Even if you never pick one up, you can't get past those headlines at the supermarket without noticing at least a few of the more outrageous claims. I believe such publications survive not because people have inquiring minds, but because they are always on the lookout for a little variety and excitement.

If you've ever been a cop or a private investigator, though, the garish headlines eventually lose their shock value. After you've spent a few years of listening to the kind of complaints filed by the general public and the lies told by those trying to evade arrest, the tabloid headlines can look pretty tame. One popular and recurring theme in the tabloids, however, sometimes crops up in genuine police work.

From time to time there will be a story about a set of twins or other siblings who were separated early in life, then ran into each other after thirty or forty years, only to discover that their lives have run an almost parallel course. Sometimes the parties will have even married spouses with the same name and drive the same make of car.

These so-called coincidences occur more frequently than you might imagine. Most cops or private investigators can remember at least one case involving encounters between individuals that *seemed* beyond the range of chance, but for which there was really no other explanation.

Cops usually shrug off such cases, because that's what cops tend to do when a thing cannot be proved one way or another. And why should cops or investigators be expected to know and understand the fine points of heredity versus environment when those who earn their living doing research can't make up their own minds? There has been an ongoing debate among scientists on the subject ever since the mechanics of human heredity were first uncovered in the nineteenth century. Just exactly how much power do genes, as opposed to social forces present in the environment, have over human behavior?

It's a controversial subject because it overflows the narrow confines of scientific method and raises big questions in fields ranging from philosophy and religion to politics and law enforcement and even medicine. Those who believe in free will, for example, have difficulty accepting the idea that behavioral traits such as overeating, aggressiveness, mental illness, or even criminality might be passed down through the generations. Those who assume that behavior can be influenced by heredity have a hard time knowing what to do with the idea of free will.

Most police officers, at least the ones I know, lean toward favoring heredity as the dominant factor in human behavior. Sometimes officers will use the term "bad seed" in reference to a second- or third-generation career criminal. Social workers, on the other hand, will usually point out that if a person is raised in a criminal household, he or she will never know another way of life.

I don't know the answer. I tend to believe heredity and environment are both important in determining human behavior. In my work of reuniting people, however, I have run across enough evidence to make me believe that heredity is a powerful factor.

One such case involved a woman who had given up her daughter for adoption almost twenty years earlier. The case was an object lesson for me, a reminder that no matter how long you stay in the business of tracking people, there will always be a story that seems more bizarre than the one you heard yesterday.

This particular case came to me by phone from a woman I never met. As a matter of fact, it was never really *my* case as such, because she didn't actually hire me. I just gave her some advice. So although there was no way for me to verify the validity of the story, I couldn't disprove it, either. And I think it was a true story for two reasons.

First, the woman had absolutely no reason to lie to me. And second, after so many years of doing the kind of work I do, I have learned to detect the ring of truth in a story, just as a dealer in precious metal can distinguish the sound made by real gold when a coin is bounced on a wooden table.

Judge for yourself.

∼ ∼ ∼

"This is Norma Tillman," I said when I answered the phone. "How may I help you?" I put aside the file I was reading. It had been a long day and there was no end in sight.

"I heard about you through a mutual friend, and I need some help." There was slight tremor in the caller's voice, as if it had taken a lot of courage for her to dial the phone, and a sadness that stood out even to a person who has talked to many sad people.

"How can I be of service, Ms. . . . ?"

"Do I have to give my real name?"

I bit back an annoyed reply. People are sometimes nervous when they call strangers. "If you become a client, *yes*. Perhaps you could tell me exactly what it is you need, and it may be that you don't actually need a private investigator anyway. But I would like to have a name so I don't have to say, 'Hey, you.'"

"Call me . . ." She paused, apparently trying to think of a suitable alias. "Call me Lynn."

"All right, Lynn, tell me your story."

"Well, almost twenty years ago I gave up my daughter for adoption. I met her father my last year of high school, while working as a grocery store clerk."

I listened quietly. People have a need to explain and justify their actions, even though most of what they say has little bearing on the true matter at hand.

"He was a young salesman who came in and sort of swept me off my feet. He never knew that he had become a father. As soon as my parents learned that I was pregnant, they shipped me off to a home for unwed mothers."

She paused for a moment, and I took the opportunity to ask a question. "Do you remember the name and location of the agency that handled the adoption?"

"I'll never forget it. They only let me see my baby once." She choked back a sob. "Yes, I know. It was in my hometown, so I think that's where my baby was probably put up for adoption. I haven't been back since right after she was born."

"In that case, you need to write a letter to the agency and tell them that it's all right for them to divulge your identity, just in case your daughter is trying to find you."

"Can I force the agency to tell me who adopted her?"

"Your daughter could probably get the records opened with a court order. But unless you can show some sort of compelling reason, it would be difficult for you to do so. I'm not saying it's impossible, but it would be time-consuming and expensive."

"I can't . . . I don't have a lot of money. And my husband doesn't know about my first daughter. After she was born, my parents moved us out of state."

"Go ahead and write that letter, then. It can't hurt, and it may well be that your daughter has left a similar letter with the agency."

"Thank you," she said sadly, then hung up. There was not a lot of hope in her voice.

About a month later, the woman called again. "Ms. Tillman, this is Lynn. We talked before, remember?"

It took me a few seconds to grasp who the voice and name belonged to. I had talked to a hundred people since then. "Yes," I finally said, "you were looking for your daughter."

"And I found her! She lives less than a mile from where I did when I was growing up. I just wanted to let you know how much your help meant to me."

"That's wonderful, Lynn. I'm happy for you." It was cases like Lynn's that finally convinced me to write *How to Find Almost Anyone, Anywhere*. There are so many cases where a person already has at hand the resources to locate a loved one but doesn't know it. My files are now filled with such testimonials.

"You don't know the half of it. Marcia—that's my daughter's name—filed her letter to the adoption agency just *two days* before I filed mine. It's like we're on the same wavelength.

"We exchanged pictures and—would you believe it—Marcia looks like my clone. We even wear our hair the same way and shop for our clothes at the same stores! In fact, we were wearing identical blouses in the pictures we exchanged."

"That's amazing, Lynn. But it's not unheard of. Relatives separated for years, especially mothers and daughters and siblings, often have similar tastes even when they've never met."

"There's more! She's attending community college, and her major is art. My major was textile design. And guess what else?"

"What, Lynn?" I smiled to myself. Her joy was infectious. Lynn sounded nothing like the sad woman who had first called.

"Marcia is working part time for the same supermarket where I met her father. I'm telling you, it's uncanny!"

"When are you going to meet your daughter?" I asked.

"Well, we've both decided that for the time being at least, we're going to take things slow. You know, kind of become pals. We have a lot of catching up to do."

"That sounds very wise," I told her. "Keep me updated."

"I will," she said brightly. "And once again, thanks!"

For the rest of the day, I had a smile on my face. Calls and letters like Lynn's are the real payoff for me. You can't buy satisfaction. I had not, however, heard the last of Lynn.

"Norma Tillman. How may I help you?"

"Ms. Tillman, this is Lynn. I need to talk with you." The bright, cheery woman who had last called a few weeks earlier had once more vanished. The sad woman was back.

"All right, Lynn. I'm listening. You haven't fallen out with Marcia, have you? That happens sometimes when relationships are renewed. It's caused by emotional strain, and it usually doesn't last long."

"Oh no! We're becoming closer than ever."

"Good," I told her.

"This *is* about Marcia, though."

"Tell me what's going on." Sometimes I feel more like a social worker than a detective. But it all comes with the territory.

"Marcia has confided in me that she's having an affair with a married man," Lynn said.

"When did she first tell you this?"

"About three weeks ago."

"Well, she's certainly not the first young woman to fall into that trap," I said. "Most recover from it and learn a lesson."

"No, this is different. *Really* different."

"How?" I asked.

"Well, to begin with, he's an older man. She met him when he came into the store where she works. He's a salesman for a food distributor."

"Well, there's another parallel between you and Marcia," I said. "One more coincidence."

"That's still not all of the story," Lynn suddenly sobbed.

"Is she pregnant?" I asked, thinking how ironic it would be if such were the case.

"No. She's not pregnant—not yet, at least."

"Well, what *is* wrong then?" I was becoming puzzled. I waited for her to pull herself together.

"When she first told me that she was in love with a tall salesman named Charles," Lynn said, "I just laughed and told Marcia that we had three more things in common—that her father's name was also Charles, that he had earned his living as a salesman, and that he was very tall. It was two weeks before she finally let his *last* name slip."

Little alarm bells had already begun to go off in my head. I saw where the story was going, but I didn't want to think about it.

"Lynn, don't tell me—"

"Yes," she blurted, "Marcia is having an affair with her own father." She began to cry softly. For a moment, I was too stunned to speak. Finally, I cleared my throat.

"Have you told her?"

"No." Lynn paused to blow her nose. "I'm afraid it will destroy our relationship if I tell her."

"But you have to do *something*. What if—"

"I know. I know. It's become a nightmare—like something from a horror movie. If Marcia had a baby with him, it would be her daughter *and* her . . . sister.

"I guess . . ." Lynn went on, "well, what I'm probably going to do is go back home, look up Charles, and tell *him* what the situation is. Won't it be a shock, though? To learn in one day that he has a grown daughter he never knew about—and that his daughter is also his mistress."

She began to cry again. I waited until she was once more under control.

"Whatever you do, Lynn, you need to do it now."

"I know."

"Will you let me know what happens, or if there's anything I can do?"

"Yes, I will." There was a click at the other end of the line.

Lynn never did get back to me, though. I don't know why. Many times through the years I have thought about Lynn's story, turning over all the details in my mind. There are logical explanations for the horrible trick fate had played on the parties involved. But they *do* stretch the imagination, don't they?

Charles was a salesman of various foods, so it was logical that he would be in grocery stores on a regular basis. It's even understandable that Marcia, growing up in the same neighborhood as her mother, would seek and find employment with one of the area's largest supermarkets.

Speaking from an objective point of view—though it's hard to be objective—Charles was attracted to Marcia because she was so much like Lynn, the girl he had once slept with when they were both young. Maybe it's even logical that a mother and daughter would have the same taste in men.

What are the odds, though, that all those things would come together in such a bizarre manner?

Even if all the parties didn't live happily ever after, I'd still like to know what happened. I'm a detective, you know, and curiosity is one of the tools of my trade.

4

The Man with the
Turquoise Eyes

PRIVATE INVESTIGATORS like me often have a tough time persuading clients that carrying out an investigation is not as simple as most people have been led to believe.

Television and movie detectives, after all, perform great feats of deductive logic every day. A couple of obscure facts, a hunch or two, and everything falls into place. The case is *always* closed before the credits begin to roll.

The public believes what it sees on television and in the movies. And why not? It looks so *easy* on the boob tube and the big screen. But in the real world of detectives, the pieces seldom fall into place that easily. In fact, there are usually very few pieces to work with. Every investigation is part science, part intuition, and a big dollop of luck. Sometimes even the *verification* of conclusions that have been reached by painstaking legwork and intuition comes from an unusual source.

Such was certainly the case when I received a letter that began, "Dear Norma, my mother came from a very dysfunctional family. . . ."

This touching letter came from a young woman by the name of Jennifer. I soon became convinced that its opening line was a vast understatement. In fact, it would be safe to say that Jennifer's mother was likely the victim of a dysfunctional *society*.

"At age sixteen," Jennifer wrote of her mother, "she got into some minor trouble and was placed temporarily in a juvenile detention home. A counselor told my mother that she needed someone to care for and love, that someday she should have a baby. . . ."

Dysfunctional, indeed. So much neglect and injustice could easily be read between those simple, straightforward lines.

That Deborah (that's how I'll refer to Jennifer's mother) really was an unwanted child seems borne out by the fact that she ended up in a juvenile facility over "minor trouble," which could easily have been a cry for help. A caring family, we can assume, would have been there to take her home.

It may well have been that the counselor at the juvenile facility was the first adult to show her any kindness or concern, even though the advice seems less than responsible. In fact, that advice given to the sixteen-year-old is enough to make a modern counselor, or even today's educated layman, shudder at the possible repercussions. The world, as we know all too well today, has an overabundance of children conceived as a solution to loneliness and neglect.

And that is exactly what happened. The counselor's suggestion, however innocently put to her, apparently took root in Deborah's mind. The impressionable girl became convinced that having a baby was the *only* way for her to acquire someone to care for and love.

Maybe the counselor qualified what she told her young client. Maybe the suggestion that a baby would be the solution to her problem of loneliness was an isolated comment taken out of context. Maybe Deborah's mother only *thought* the counselor said that. Who can say for sure after all these years?

Whatever was really *said*, however, doesn't matter now. What Deborah *heard* was the part about having a baby to love and care for. It was apparently still clear in her mind, not long afterward, when she went to stay with relatives in a town far from her home.

In her new surroundings, Deborah found someone, at least

temporarily, to hold her and offer shelter and comfort from a cold, unfeeling world.

"He was a nice man," Deborah had told her daughter many years later, but by then she had forgotten so many details about him. He had been several years older than Deborah, going through a divorce at the time of their affair, and had "three beautiful daughters"—Jennifer's half-sisters.

The most vivid memory of all, though, was Deborah's memory of Bill's eyes. They were a beautiful shade of turquoise, unlike any eyes she had ever seen before.

"Wouldn't it be nice," Deborah remembered thinking, "to have a daughter with eyes like his?"

"My mother became pregnant," Jennifer continued in her letter nearly twenty-five years later. The letter ended with a heart-wrenching plea for help. "I think it is time I found my father and met my half-sisters. Because none of them knows I exist, I do not know how to approach them or how to handle the situation so that I do not hurt anyone."

I had only a few facts with which to begin my search: Bill's real name, the place where Deborah had met him, the probability that he had been divorced, and not least of all, as it would turn out, the unusual color of his eyes. In the course of my career, I had followed delicate strings of evidence with far fewer facts. But finding Bill, I knew, would be the easy part. The hard part would be bringing him together with a daughter he didn't know existed.

If Bill was even still alive, it was possible that he had established another family. What would the consequences be if a second wife were to find out that her husband had produced a daughter out of wedlock? Or what if Bill was in fragile health and unable to deal with such a shocking revelation?

The worse-case scenario that I could think of, however, the one calculated to cause the most pain, would be for Bill simply to deny having had a relationship with Jennifer's mother and refuse to speak to his daughter.

I have seen all these scenarios in my career. Though they are not the usual outcome, the possibility of such an unhappy ending always haunts me in cases like these. I've decided that a little bit of trepidation is good. It makes me careful in approaching people, reminding me that the happy endings I work for depend on skillful human relations as well as skillful investigations.

With a little apprehension, then, and a lot of hope, I began my search in the courthouse of the jurisdiction where Deborah had met the mysterious Bill. As sometimes happens, I quickly hit pay dirt. The divorce decree (considered a public document in most jurisdictions) yielded a date of birth for Bill, his address at the time of the divorce, and a Social Security number. Armed with these new facts, I fired up one of the three computers that I use in my work and quickly came up with a current driver's license, a vehicle registration number, and a last known address.

Now the easy part was over. The hard part was still ahead. Somewhat nervously I dialed the phone, hoping for the best. I'm always just a little nervous when I make these calls.

"Is this Bill?" I asked when a deep voice answered on the other end.

"Yes, what can I do for you?"

"My name is Norma Tillman. I'm a private investigator, and I need to talk to you about a *very* personal matter. . . ."

~ ~ ~

A few days later, on national television, Jennifer met her father and her three half-sisters for the first time. Because my investigation had been conducted over the phone and by mail, this was also the first time I had met any of them.

It was a tearful, joyous meeting, as might be expected. And as they all hugged and kissed Jennifer, it was obvious to me, at least, that this was not a case where genetic testing would be needed to establish family ties. For one thing, there was an amazing resemblance between Jennifer and her youngest half-sister. The same curly dark hair and uptilted nose, the same cupid's-bow lips. And I could see points of resemblance with the other girls as well—a dimpled cheek, a petite figure, a distinctive walk. But the most compelling evidence was in Jennifer's eyes. Not the expression of joy, but the eyes themselves.

"Yes," I wrote in my investigative notes after seeing my client and her father in person for the first time, "Jennifer has the most beautiful turquoise eyes—just like her father's."

5

Undercover

"WHEN IN ROME, do as the Romans do," the axiom advises. And as with most old sayings, there's a lot of truth in that one. (If there weren't, why would we still be repeating it?)

In my line of work, the ability to blend in can sometimes mean the difference between success and failure. Although I usually find it most effective to be up front with my investigations—and I always make a point to stay within the law—there are still times when I need to remain anonymous. And then I find it invaluable not only to *do* as the Romans do but also to dress the part.

I'm not talking about the trench coat with collar turned up and the fedora pulled down over my eyes. Fifty years ago, when the popular fictional image of the hard-boiled private eye was established, people dressed in such a manner would have been unobtrusive—which is why Philip Marlowe and Mike Hammer dressed that way. But the trench coats in my closet are almost entirely for publicity shots. For my actual undercover work, I employ a variety of costumes, wigs, and other devices to change my appearance whenever I need to. At various times I have made myself into a glamorous world traveler, a secretary on lunch break, a pregnant woman (with the help of a fanny pack turned to the front), and other characters too numerous to mention. Needless to say, some personas are easier to adopt than others. One of the most memorable involved a case in the Deep South.

35

"How can I help you, Mr. Belden?" I took a sip of tea from the exquisite porcelain cup the housekeeper had set before me. "I'm sure it must be important since you were willing to fly me in from Nashville just to see if I might take your case. There are plenty of investigators here."

"You come highly recommended," Mr. Belden replied. He was a tall, slightly stooped man with white hair and skin that had taken on the translucence of age. At one time, the buildings he designed had been the talk of the national architectural community. "Discretion will be very important in this matter," he warned.

"I keep secrets for a living, Mr. Belden."

"I know, I know. I didn't mean to imply otherwise. My sources tell me that you specialize in finding lost people. They also assure me that even after you find lost people, you won't divulge their whereabouts unless they agree to it."

"That's true. I think it would be irresponsible to work any other way."

"You must lose a lot of money with your ethical position on that matter," he said.

"I do all right," I assured him.

"I see." He nodded his head as if he had come to a decision. "Ms. Tillman, my wife is dying. We don't know how long she has left, but it probably won't be more than a month or so."

"I'm very sorry," I quietly told him.

"Don't get me wrong," he continued. "We've both lived long and prosperous lives. We can't complain. The only thing is, I'd like for my wife to be able to die with a satisfied mind. Right now, she's deeply disturbed."

"What can I do to help, Mr. Belden?" My natural suspicion had subsided. He was obviously not a man out to cause anyone harm.

"My wife already had a daughter when we married. I raised her just like my own. Trudy was a bright, happy child until she was fifteen." He paused for a moment, as if reflecting on times past. "What do you know about schizophrenia?"

"Not much," I admitted.

"It's a horrible disease, Ms. Tillman. It robs people of their dignity and sometimes their freedom. When Trudy first became ill, there were still a lot of doctors who blamed parents for schizophrenic children. We knew better, though, and we cared for her the best we could."

"I can imagine how difficult it must have been."

"Yes, it was and is difficult. Trudy was in and out of hospitals for twenty-five years. A couple of years ago, she was started on an experimental drug that has brought relief to a lot of people. At first the results were promising. Then she fell apart again, and it looked as if we were going to have to hospitalize her once more," he sighed.

"Trudy hates hospitals. She's always been afraid that one day she would be locked up and never be allowed outside again. So she got frightened at the prospect of another hospitalization and left in the middle of the night.

"We were worried sick because we knew Trudy didn't have much money with her. When she finally called, we were so relieved that we made a deal with her. We promised her a monthly check to live on. The check was to be sent to a post-office box in Washington State. And we gave our word that we wouldn't try to find her, if she would promise to call if she got in trouble.

"That was nearly two years ago. We've kept our side of the bargain. But now my wife is dying, and she's worried about Trudy's welfare."

"Has Trudy been cashing her checks?"

"Yes, every month. But Abigail is afraid that someone may be taking advantage of Trudy, spending all her money. She has always been such a trusting person; it would be easy for someone to take advantage of her."

"Why don't you just put a letter in with the check and have her write back?"

"We've done that. But there's been no response. I want you to go to Washington and check on her. But she mustn't know who you are. She might *really* vanish if she found out."

"Mr. Belden, almost any private detective could do this job. I work alone, and if I take several days off from my business, it's going to cost me a lot of money. I'll have to charge you quite a bit to make up the difference. Why don't you just contact one of the big detective agencies that has a branch in Washington State?"

"No, I want *you* to do it—especially now that I've talked to you. If I bring in someone who looks like a television detective, my wife won't believe anything she's told. I think she'll believe you."

My impulse was to turn him down. This would be a very time-consuming job. Looking at the hopeful expression in his eyes, though, I was unable to tell him no. "All right, Mr. Belden. I'll do it. I can fly out tomorrow."

Trudy had taken up residency in a mid-size coastal town. It was a sort of storybook place, a quaint little city surrounded by green forests. I caught a shuttle from Seattle to the tiny regional airport, where I rented an unwashed compact Chevrolet so as not to draw attention to myself as I might with a luxury car.

I already knew Trudy's address before I arrived. She had used a credit card twice for small purchases and had put her real Social Security number on an application for credit at a downtown department store. Most of us—and mostly without knowing it—leave a trail of paper that can be followed by professional trackers like me, as surely as Daniel Boone could follow a bear through the forest. Picking up the scent is a learned skill, but it's not all that difficult.

A quick drive through the neighborhood confirmed my suspicion that Trudy was not living in the most exclusive part of the city. The buildings and houses were rundown, though they retained a kind of Victorian charm. Here and there, tired-looking men and women sat on front stoops, watching the traffic go by, and in one alley a bag lady rummaged through a garbage can.

I made a note of the building that Trudy had listed as her address on the credit application. Then I went to find a motel nearby. There I laid out some old jeans, a patched, much-washed chambray shirt that I had brought for the occasion—so I could dress like the Romans—and a faded old windbreaker that I wore on chilly days when I didn't have to venture far from my house. I found a convenience store and bought a few drinks and snacks—supplies for my stakeout. Because night was falling, I decided to begin my work early the next morning.

As the sun came up, I hastily donned my undercover wardrobe and pointed the rental car toward Trudy's neighborhood. As the day wore on, I moved my car several times when people began to look too closely at me. Nobody even remotely resembling Trudy's picture had emerged from the building all day, though it was obvious that several people inhabited it.

The picturesque brick structure appeared to have once been a store building, perhaps one of the family groceries that used to dot the country in an America before shopping centers and supermarkets. Judging by the people coming and going, it had been subdivided into several different apartments.

Suddenly, as I watched, lights blinked on in a corner room on the second floor of Trudy's building. Someone parted the sheer curtains and looked out briefly, and I got the distinct impression of a little girl with her hair in pigtails. As I continued to stare, the person in that apartment began to pace back and forth.

Adjusting my small binoculars, I took a closer look at the lighted apartment. The curtains remained partially opened, so I had a clear view of the delicate-looking woman within. What had looked like pigtails were really two ponytails drawn up on each side of her head. A ruffled white blouse completed the little-girl look. Even through the field glasses, I could see that the woman in the apartment was the same person as the one in the photograph tucked away in the file folder beside me.

Putting down the field glasses, I took out my camera and adjusted the telephoto lens. A moment later I had pictures that I knew would reassure Trudy's mother once I had them enlarged to eight-by-tens.

Two hours later, Trudy was still pacing the floor, so I went back to my motel room. By now I was convinced that she didn't get out a lot. And I couldn't wait around forever; my list of things to do was getting longer every hour. If I wanted to get closer to Trudy, I would have to use a different strategy.

I tracked down the landlord and rented a room in Trudy's building, for a nominal daily fee. I opened the door to my room and was surprised to find that it was immaculate, with a sort of Lysol smell hanging in the air. There was nothing in the unfurnished room, but I hoped I wouldn't be there long enough to need much anyway.

By my reckoning, I was next door to Trudy's room, which was right beside the small communal kitchen. There was also a communal bathroom down the hall. Both were shabby but clean.

The elderly woman who rented the room to me had explained the rules about not touching anyone else's food. Then she had warned me that the rule was often broken. And the aromas permeating the hallway stood as evidence that the rule forbidding cooking in the rooms was not enforced. The odor of cooking cabbage attested to covert hot plates and electric skillets. Apparently the apartment building was run on a live-and-let-live basis.

As Spartan as the building was, I knew that only the aristocracy of the street people, the elite of the down-and-out, had enough money to rent a room there. It was a big step above missions and immensely better than sleeping on the streets.

I decided to go downstairs and meet my neighbors, wondering whether my car parked six blocks away on a commercial lot would be all right. I shrugged to myself. There was no use worrying about what was beyond my control.

Sitting on the front stoop, trying to blend in, I was startled by a booming voice: "Hello there. I believe you're new here."

"Yes," I replied, somewhat suspiciously. He was a small man, shabbily but cleanly dressed, who seemed to be smiling from the inside out, though his broken teeth and the scars around his eyes suggested that he had not always been pleasant.

"I'm Jack. Some call me Brother Jack. I look after people round here. I just wanted to let you know that if you need anything, or if anyone bothers you, give me a yell. Everybody knows that Brother Jack takes care of the people on this block."

"Well, I—"

"Excuse me," he said, looking beyond me as I offered a handshake. "Jonesy, you old scoundrel! When did you get out?" Jack grabbed a big bear of a man who had walked up the sidewalk and hugged him like an old friend.

"They give me my walkin' papers yesterday," the big man said.

"You got a place to stay?"

"No, I was hopin' I'd run into an old cellmate," the man said with a rueful smile.

"Well, it just so happens you did. Come on, I'll take to you meet the man at the mission. We need to start getting you on your feet again before you fall into your old habits."

Jack turned once more before leaving. "And don't *you* forget, either. You need *anything*, just look up Brother Jack."

I watched Brother Jack, the self-ordained protector of those on the streets, as he walked the big man down the block, all the while talking in an animated fashion. His would be an interesting story. I was sorry I wouldn't have time to hear it.

A little later, I went back upstairs to my room, took out a clean newspaper I had lifted from the top of the wastebasket in the kitchen, and tried to focus on the words while listening for Trudy to open her door. After an hour or so, I spread the paper out on the cheap carpet to make a bed, wadded my windbreaker up into a pillow, and drifted off to sleep.

The next morning, the coffee smelled wonderful as I dropped a dollar in the little basket that said COFFEE AND CAKE MONEY and helped myself to one of the small cellophane-wrapped cakes. I filled one of the Styrofoam cups with coffee and sat down at the little kitchen table. I was taking my first sip when Trudy opened the door to her room and emerged with a small coffeepot in her hand. She nodded shyly, then went to the sink and rinsed out the pot before filling it with water.

Glancing through her open door, I saw that she had a refrigerator and a small electric grill. The room was tastefully furnished, neat, and clean. In the middle of the floor was a tiny table standing on spread-out newspapers, obviously in the process of being refinished. I slid my hand into my jeans pocket and turned on the tiny microcassette recorder. An amplifier concealed under my blue chambray shirt was capable of picking up the tiniest whisper in the room.

"Hi," I said. "I'm Norma."

Trudy turned off the faucet and faced me, eyes downcast, the small pot of water in her hand. Up close, she looked her age, nearly forty. But the little-girl look I had noted from the street was even more pronounced close up. With her pigtails and pinafore, she reminded me of Dorothy in *The Wizard of Oz*. It was as if she had decided to go back to a happier time in her life—a time when she was about twelve years old.

"I'm Trudy," she finally responded.

"Have you lived here long?" I asked. "I just got here yesterday."

"I've been here a little while," she answered, then started toward the door.

"It's kind of lonely being in a new town," I offered.

"I don't mind. I kind of like it," she replied. "Sometimes people want to get *too* close. They can smother you."

"That's true," I said, standing as Trudy edged toward the door. "But maybe you could show me the neighborhood later today."

"I don't think so. I have work to do today. I don't like to get behind in my work."

"You're painting that table, I see. It looks really good."

She glanced at me with wary eyes, and I quickly backed away. My instructions had been explicit. She was not to become suspicious of me.

"Well, some other time," I said, turning to open the door to my room. "Nice to meet you."

Her door closed softly, and I heard the lock click into place. She had disappeared without saying another word to me. And I didn't really need to hear more. My mission was finished. I had pictures and a recording to reassure her mother that everything was all right—at least as well as it would ever be for a woman in Trudy's situation. I found myself admiring her for the relatively stable life she had put together for herself against the odds.

Two days later, sitting at the large mahogany desk in his study, Mr. Belden wrote out a check. Abigail Belden, eyes red-rimmed and hollow, had grasped my hand and wept in gratitude when I showed her the pictures of her daughter and played the recording for her.

Now he extended the check, and I sat and stared at it for a moment.

"What's wrong, Ms. Tillman?"

"I just hate to take so much money from you."

"It's what I agreed to pay, isn't it?"

"Yes," I replied.

"Ms. Tillman, a lack of money is one problem I don't have. And money couldn't buy the peace of mind you have given Abigail and me," he said.

"Go along now," he added. "The check I just wrote to you is by far the best bargain I ever received from anyone."

And I could tell by his eyes that he really meant it. Years later, I still feel good when I think about the expression on his face that day.

6

Where True Love Waits

IF YOU THINK romance is dead in twentieth-century America, sit down and have a chat with a private investigator. On any given day, thousands of men and women walk into the offices of private detectives, ready to lay out big bucks in the name of love.

Not long ago, in the comedy film *Honeymoon in Vegas*, Nicholas Cage played a private investigator who inadvertently lost his girlfriend in a rigged poker game to a professional gambler. The plot centered on Cage's attempts to get his fiancée back from the gambler, who had become convinced that the young woman was the reincarnation of his dead wife. But a hilarious subplot was dedicated to a balding, insecure little man who wanted Cage to provide proof of his wife's alleged infidelities.

The humor stemmed, to a large degree, from the man's belief that his wife was having an affair with none other than former heavyweight champion Mike Tyson—who was locked away in prison at the time. Cage's client even had a picture of his wife with the imprisoned prizefighter. To everyone except Cage's client, it was obvious that the picture had been crudely doctored and that his colleagues were behind the scheme to make him jealous. Nothing anyone could tell him would sway the little man's belief that Mike Tyson was sleeping with his wife.

Though meant to be humorous, that particular character accurately reflects some of the distraught men and women who seek out private investigators when their love lives go awry.

Some, like the little man in *Honeymoon in Vegas*, are simply insecure people who don't trust anyone. Others have genuine reasons
for believing that their mates have strayed.

A colleague of mine once recounted the story of a wealthy
businessman who became convinced that his wife was having an
affair. He hired my colleague, who taught him how to attach a
device to his own phone and record telephone conversations
between the woman and her lover. Although it was obvious that
they were making coded references to illicit liaisons, neither ever
called the other by a real name.

After a while, the businessman decided to take a closer interest
in his wife's affairs. He actually began to go places with her, listening for that voice he had become so familiar with. As they were
leaving church one Sunday, the man finally heard *the* voice. It
belonged to the pastor of the church he and his wife had attended
for years. The divorce happened in short order, the pastor was
expelled in disgrace, and my colleague collected a healthy fee.
With such things going on every day, how can anyone say that
romance is dead?

All right, so that isn't the way you want to think of romance.
And I have to admit I don't like it much either. Clandestine photographs and intimate recordings are not exactly the stuff of
which true love is made. But they *are*, sad though it may seem,
the concerns that preoccupy a large segment of the average private detective's clientele. I never actively sought to specialize in
divorce cases, but sometimes I have taken them when money was
short. I've seen enough marriages gone bad, enough love affairs
turned sour, to become just a little jaded about love.

So you can imagine how thrilled I was one day when a woman
walked into my office and asked for my help in finding a long-lost
love. Her story sounded just like the plot of a movie. I could
almost smell the magnolias and hear the violins.

"How can I help you?" I pushed aside the file on my desk and
looked the woman over—discreetly, of course, with the kind of
covert examination that becomes second nature to cops and good

investigators. A skilled student of human nature can learn volumes about people simply by taking note of the way they dress, speak, and carry themselves.

The woman in my office that day appeared to be of good breeding. Her clothes were elegant but understated, and she carried about her an air of refinement. In her late forties or early fifties, she had aged well. She spoke with a subtle accent that I couldn't place. She seemed to be having trouble getting started, so I gently prompted her. After all, it had to be a strain on a woman of obvious culture to come to the office of a private investigator.

"I know it's not easy to tell your secrets to a stranger," I said with a smile. "But I promise that whatever you say to me stays with me."

"Well . . . it *is* a little embarrassing," she fluttered. "You see, I want to find a man from my past."

My ears perked up as I reached for a pad and pencil. People expect you to take notes. It gives them confidence that you are really paying attention.

"What was your relationship to this man?" I asked.

"He was my husband."

"How long has it been since you've seen him?"

"Thirty-five years." She took out a dainty lavender handkerchief and began to twist it nervously in her hands.

"Well, you should certainly have enough information on an ex-husband to give me a place to start, even after so many years. What was your husband's date of birth?"

"I'm not sure."

For a moment, I looked at the woman with a question in my eyes, but she glanced away. It seemed odd for her to forget such a thing. In my experience, I have found that women rarely forget birthdays and anniversaries.

"Perhaps I should give you some background," the woman said apologetically. "This wasn't your ordinary marriage."

"What do you mean?"

"Well, we were married by proxy."

By proxy? I had, of course, heard of such marriages, but I had never actually encountered one. The woman twisted her handkerchief again and went on.

"It was an arranged marriage. My family had come to America before his. You see, we were betrothed as children. His family was still in the old country when we reached the proper age to be married.

"Even though the plans had already been made for his family to arrive not long after the day our wedding had been set, our parents went ahead and had the marriage by proxy at the proper time, because it was the traditional thing to do. I had never actually seen my fiancé—not after I was old enough to remember."

"Were you agreeable to an arranged marriage?" I asked, thoroughly intrigued.

"Well, I didn't know any better. It was the way things had always been. I just accepted it. Besides, when I saw him for the first time. . . ." Her voice trailed off, and for a second she looked like a young, flustered girl with stars in her eyes.

"He was more than you expected?" I nudged her on.

"Oh, *much* more than I expected. He was so handsome. I fell in love at first sight with the young man I was already married to."

A love story, I thought to myself, *a genuine love story. Not a case of a woman who wants her husband followed. Not a jealous woman looking for a bigger divorce settlement. A real romance.* A few stars were gleaming in my own eyes I'm sure.

"Well, obviously you didn't live happily ever after. What happened to separate you?" I was genuinely curious.

"Oh, my family had suffered a few financial setbacks by the time he and his family arrived. It was just a matter of money. My father couldn't come through with the dowry he had promised. His father demanded an annulment. Because we had never consummated the marriage, it wasn't a difficult thing."

"Were you and your husband consulted?"

"No, not really. We were there when the discussions were going on, but nobody asked our opinion."

Tears were just about to overflow from the woman's eyes, which she dabbed with the handkerchief.

"Did you and he ever get a chance to talk alone?"

"Oh, yes, we talked quite a bit. The negotiations went on for a long time. I was madly in love with him from the moment I first saw him."

"And how did he feel?" I asked.

"Well, of course, being from the old country, we had both been trained not to show our true feelings. I knew, though . . . as a woman, I just *knew* that he loved me as much as I loved him."

"That's a very touching story," I told her.

"All these years I've wondered about the man who was my husband for such a short time. I remarried, of course, but even when I was being a faithful wife, I'd sometimes think of him.

"And now, my husband is dead, my children are grown, and both my parents have passed away. I want to find out, once and for all, if he felt the same way about me as I felt about him."

She paused and looked me directly in the eyes for the first time. "Do you think I'm being foolish?"

"Of course not. I hope I'd do exactly the same thing if I were in your situation."

"Let me write you a check so that you can get started right away," she said brightly.

A romantic woman, and one with money in the bank—a rare combination indeed! I was so caught up in the story that I had forgotten to mention my fee, I quickly brought myself back to reality.

"All right," I cleared my throat. "Tell me everything you can remember about your ex-husband. No matter how trivial you may think a detail is, it may mean the difference between success and failure."

It was not an easy task that had been set before me. The name of my client's ex-husband was a common one—at least the

Anglicized family name that his parents had adopted. I traveled down dead-end road after dead-end road.

My client could provide no Social Security number and no exact date of birth, only a range of years. A search of divorce records in the city where my client had lived came up blank, leaving me to suspect that the marriage between the two young people had been of a religious and cultural, rather than a legal, nature. After exhausting all the channels through which I normally search, I still had a long, intimidating list of names.

From time to time, my client would call. There would always be just a hint of sadness as she inquired about my progress. I was beginning to feel like the Grinch in the *Grinch Who Stole Christmas*, a private detective who couldn't even unite starstruck lovers. Then my client called with a bit of information, something she had remembered as she was looking at some of her old pictures. Her prince charming, she recalled, had been interested in studying pediatrics and had been fascinated with the Rocky Mountains. Maybe, just maybe. . . .

Within an hour, I had narrowed my search to three individual pediatricians, all practicing in Colorado and Utah. Nervously, I dialed the first number and introduced myself to the puzzled man at the other end, then launched hopefully into my questions.

"Sir, can you tell me if you immigrated to the United States about thirty-five years ago?"

"Yes, I did. What's this all about?" He sounded cautious, and understandably so.

"Were you married by proxy to a young woman already living here?"

There was dead quiet for a moment before he replied, his voice tight. "Yes, I was married by proxy before my arrival."

"Just out of curiosity, are you married now?"

"No, I'm not." The voice was now edging toward hostile. "My wife has been deceased for a while. If you don't tell me what this is about, I'm going to hang up."

"It just so happens that I represent—" I paused dramatically, then told him my client's name. Once more there was dead silence—not the reaction I had expected from a man who had just been tracked down at the request of a lovely woman who remembered him fondly after so many years.

"Did you understand what I said, sir? Your ex-wife is eager to see you again."

Still more silence.

"Sir . . . are you still there?"

"Have you told her where I am?" he asked, obviously angry.

"No, I was going to call her after I confirmed your identity."

"Whatever she's paying you, I'll pay you double to keep my location a secret from her. Under no circumstance do I want that woman to know where I am. Do you understand?"

"Yes," I answered. "I understand." I was so shocked by his response that I didn't even become indignant that he had offered me money to betray my client. I respect the privacy of those I track down. All he had to do was tell me he didn't want to see my client. But before I could say anything to reassure him, the upset man slammed down the receiver.

She took a seat across from me, as demure and dignified as ever. I was not looking forward to telling her that her Romeo, the man of her innermost fantasies, did not share her feelings. Wanting to have the tears dried quickly, I came right out with it.

"I've found your ex-husband. I'm very sorry, but he has asked me not to tell you where he is."

For a moment she sat quietly without speaking. Then she wordlessly took out a small pad from her purse and scribbled something on it. At first, I thought she was writing a message because she was too upset to speak.

She ripped it from the pad and handed it to me. On the

paper she had written a man's name, a date, and a Social Security number.

"This one shouldn't be so hard to find," she told me.

"Who is *this?*" I asked, wondering how we had gone from one subject to another so quickly.

"He's an old boyfriend. Since my ex-husband doesn't want to see me, I'd like for you to find this man."

"I'll see what I can do," was my stunned reply.

She smiled and left the office without further comment, without even having asked if her ex-husband by proxy had given a reason for his refusal to see her. Maybe she already knew the answer.

When I found the old boyfriend, his desire to remain hidden from my client was as adamant as that of her ex-husband. I think I was more disappointed than my client. And I never did find out why her former loves were so determined to remain unfound.

7

Mission Accomplished

"MY NAME IS Robert Sutherland. My call is in reference to a debt of honor I owe to a fallen comrade in Vietnam. . . ."

The message, left on my answering machine, went on to say that any help I could give would be very much appreciated. It was a haunting message, like a voice from another century, from an era when such terms as "debt of honor" actually meant something. Before I ever met the man who had identified himself as Robert Sutherland, I knew I was going to help him if I could.

I immediately made arrangements for a flight to upstate New York, where Robert Sutherland had settled after the Vietnam War. Somehow I knew that the investigation upon which I was about to embark would be special, one of those I'd never forget.

The next day, in a rental car, I drove down the New York back roads, following directions I had gotten from the local postmaster. When I found the house that had been described to me, it seemed to fit well with the voice that had called me from so far away—isolated and lonely.

For no apparent reason, staring into the dense, somehow ominous thickets behind the house, I shivered. Minutes later the door opened, and I finally saw Robert Sutherland in person—a thin, slightly stooped, slow-moving, mustachioed man in his mid-forties, wearing a fatigue shirt. The anguish in his eyes was like a physical assault that left me wondering just how long this man had been in emotional and physical pain.

It was as if Robert Sutherland had become the prototype, the archetypal forgotten veteran of a war most would prefer to forget, a dirty little conflict that had killed more than fifty thousand young men and sucked the life out of many others of their generation without offering them even the solace of a ticker-tape parade when they returned home. Suddenly I understood my apprehension about approaching this back-woods retreat. Robert and so many others like him had been mistreated. He had a right to be angry at a society that had taken his sacrifice for granted, and I had been a part of that complacency.

"Robert," I extended my hand, staring into those haunted eyes. "My name is Norma Tillman. I'm here to help you if I can."

Lt. Martin McElroy was a man who most definitely understood terms like *courage, honor, allegiance*, and *responsibility*. The infantrymen who served under him, the gravel-pounding grunts who followed him into battle—including a sergeant by the name of Robert Sutherland—learned to love him.

A stocky, square-jawed man who stared out of his basic training photograph with a determined gaze, Martin McElroy was not much older than the troops who served under his command in a war where the average age of the basic military recruit was nineteen. He was an individual who inspired confidence in others. And he had been that way even during his youth—a young man of whom his mother once said, "We thought Martin was indestructible. We expected him to go off and win the war." Her words brought to mind a statement attributed to automaker Henry Ford: "Asking who should be in charge is like asking who should sing tenor."

What Ford meant, of course, was that the person who leads should be the person who *can* lead. Unfortunately, the actuality does not always align with the theory. In combat, there are always certain individuals to whom everyone else looks for guidance and leadership when the shooting starts. And ideally the person wearing the badge of authority is also the leader of fact. But not always—probably not even most of the time.

Every man and woman who has ever been in combat understands the dynamics of leadership, the difference between figureheads and real leaders. In fact, it may well be that the occasions on which leadership and rank of office actually come together are so rare that individuals who fit the category make a lasting impression on those whom they lead.

Martin McElroy was obviously such a man. The troops under him followed and obeyed not only because he was "officially" their commanding officer, but because he was a leader they trusted. And they followed him because he lived as one of them—down in the mud and the blood, trying to keep his feet dry and live to fight another day.

As a true leader, Lieutenant McElroy understood that you never allow a person under your command to take a risk that you yourself are not prepared to take. It was a matter of honor with him. Robert Sutherland remembered the last such incident as if it were yesterday, instead of February 28, 1966.

Three Vietcong soldiers had been killed by land mines the previous night during an attack on Charlie Company's position. Martin McElroy made the decision to go out and retrieve the bodies himself. His sergeant, Robert Sutherland, protested vehemently. He debated and argued, stopping just short of insubordination, that he and not the commanding officer should recover the bodies.

In the end, because he was a good and obedient soldier, Robert Sutherland gave in. He watched with trepidation as Lieutenant McElroy, who was not only his commander but also his friend, gingerly made his way through the field where the dragon's teeth had been sown and now waited to burst forth from the earth with fiery, murderous rage.

Suddenly, in one of those moments that emblazons itself permanently in one's memory, the ground shuddered as Lieutenant McElroy stepped on a land mine—an American land mine. Rumbling shock waves, dust, and heat went rippling out from the spot in an insane cacophony of sound, light, and the unmistakable, unforgettable odors of blood and burning cordite.

"I felt the concussion," Robert Sutherland said in a barely controlled voice on a day nearly thirty years later, a voice still filled with the anguish of that moment he had re-lived thousands of times since 1966.

"I was there to cradle him in my arms," Robert told me. "He asked me to deliver a message for him, and I promised I would."

Almost thirty years after watching his friend die an agonizing death in a remote Vietnamese field—the location of which has probably been forgotten by everyone else—Sergeant Sutherland was still trying to keep that promise.

I told him I would help him deliver the message to Lieutenant McElroy's family. Then I asked to see how much information he had on the family.

As it turned out, he didn't have much at all. Robert had searched long and diligently, but the sad fact of the matter was that he didn't know *how* to ask the right questions. The keepers of the records, wherever you find them and whatever they are called, will often give you only what you *specifically* ask for, even though they may have access to much more and even though the information is perfectly legal. It's as if such people fear squandering information the way a tightwad fears spending money. I don't know why this is so. But in my experience it's almost a defining characteristic of people in the field of record-keeping. Most are not malicious or unfeeling, but getting facts from them is often like pulling teeth. A successful private investigator is a person who has developed the ability to extract that information quickly and painlessly—sometimes before the record-keeper even realizes that a question has been asked.

In addition to his lack of experience in conducting a search,

Robert Sutherland had another impediment. He suffered from a degenerative joint disease. Every step he took, supported by metal crutches, was a new moment of intense pain to be overcome. For him, the concept of "legwork" was almost a cruel joke. I vowed to help this man if at all possible. I didn't know how, but I knew I was going to give it my best shot—no matter how long it took or how much it cost.

When my routine computer checks failed to turn up the proper information, I flew to Washington, DC, for many fruitless hours of searching through federal records. It was not until I visited the Vietnam Memorial that I found Martin McElroy's name. There it was, engraved on that magnificent wall. In the casualty directory I found an address in the small town of Munster, Indiana, where McElroy had been born. Armed with that new information, I was soon on an airplane bound for Indiana, excited that my quest—and Robert's—would soon be over. Sometimes, in moments of excitement, even those like me who know better will celebrate too soon. It didn't take me long to find out that my search was still a long way from done.

Not only was Lieutenant McElroy's family not at the listed address, but the address no longer existed. The site had been bulldozed, and a new subdivision now crowded the fourteen acres of rich farmland where the McElroy house had once stood. Communities, like people, can change a lot in thirty years. I sat in my rental car for a few minutes, almost in tears. Robert Sutherland was about to receive another disappointing report. His final mission had been delayed once more. Then I took a deep breath and reached for the car keys. Robert had been disappointed many times in thirty years. Surely I could endure a little disappointment myself as we worked toward our common goal.

Now, I realized, it was time to do a little old-fashioned detective work. So I searched out the nearest public library and dug into those sources that I share with the FBI and the CIA—public records in the form of city directories, phone books, newspaper files, and even high-school yearbooks.

In the local newspaper files I found the 1966 obituary for Lt. Martin McElroy. I had hoped there would be a different address, a new starting point. But the address given was the same as the one on the casualty list at the Vietnam Memorial.

That wasn't the end of the line, though, not by a long shot. That obituary contained other information. In fact, there was a nugget of gold buried in the midst of it, though it was not obvious at first.

None of the former neighbors nor the local McElroys knew anything about Martin or his family. "No relation at all," I was told time after time as I dialed phones or knocked on doors.

Re-reading the obituary for perhaps the twentieth time, I suddenly realized the significance of one particular piece of information. Martin McElroy's father had been employed by a large steel manufacturing company in the area. I realized the company's personnel files would have a forwarding address, a place where Martin's father's pension check would have been mailed. Even if he had died while still an active employee, they would have a record of his last address.

I threw my shoulders back and my chin up and resumed my investigation, operating under my trusty working theory that *every problem contains the seed for its own solution.* Sometimes it's hard to recognize, but it's always there. As it turned out, the company where Martin McElroy's father had been employed *was* the seed I needed to find, the missing piece that would help me solve the puzzle.

After I explained the situation, the personnel manager of the steel company provided me with the Florida address where Martin's father had been living when he died in 1986.

I was soon on a plane heading south. By the end of the day, I had met Martin McElroy's mother and explained the situation to her. When I left her apartment, I had an invitation for myself and Sgt. Robert Sutherland to attend a McElroy family reunion a few days later. I was almost as excited as Robert when I called him with the good news.

≈ ≈ ≈

It was obvious that Robert was uncomfortable on the flight bound for the reunion. In addition to his pain from joint disease that had condemned him to walking with crutches, he was visibly—and understandably—nervous. After all, Robert had spent three decades dreaming of what was about to happen.

I must admit to a few butterflies myself. I knew that sometimes the reality of things wished for and dreamed of don't quite measure up to the anticipation. I fervently hoped that Robert would not be disappointed. Somehow, though, I sensed that everything would be all right. And I knew it almost certainly at the moment when Robert Sutherland stood at the door and extended his trembling hand to Martin McElroy's mother.

"I am honored," he said, barely controlling the tremor in his voice.

Moments later, sitting on the couch, the thin, stooped Vietnam veteran with a drooping mustache and dark hollows around his eyes delivered the message that had been entrusted to him when his legs were still straight, at a time when walking was not an agonizing ordeal.

"I served with your son very honorably and very proudly for his time in Vietnam." Robert paused to swallow the lump in his throat. "I was with him at the instant of his death. And he asked me to tell you that he loved you very much. For thirty years—almost—I've kept looking.

"I'm so proud, so pleased, and so honored to be able to tell you that you were the last thought on his mind. Martin McElroy brought nothing but credit to this family. He was the most valuable person I ever knew."

By the time Robert finished speaking, silence hung in the room—the shared silence of a sacred moment. And most who were there, I believe, felt that somewhere and somehow, Martin McElroy knew that his final message had at long last been delivered. But there was one final stop before Robert Sutherland would be able to relax fully.

Dressed in camouflage combat fatigues and a military beret, his decorations bright on his chest, Sgt. Robert Sutherland approached the gravesite where Lt. Martin McElroy lay at rest. He walked slowly and haltingly, but with obvious determination.

For the occasion, Robert had put aside his metal crutches. In his left hand was a wooden cane he needed for support. But his right hand had to be free for the final stage of his mission.

Facing the grave and the monument, he came to attention. Just for a brief moment you could see the young man who had gone off to war, bright-eyed and idealistic, as he brought up his right hand in a crisp military salute.

"Sir!" he shouted. "Sergeant Sutherland reporting. Mission accomplished!"

Later, Robert sat talking quietly. There was a look of peace on his face that had been missing before.

"I have the feeling that I'll be able to take a long, deep breath and relax for maybe the first time in thirty years."

The old soldier paused for a moment as if staring off into a place only he could see. His eyes had lost their haunted look. He seemed almost content. Then he went on.

"It's like a poem I found a couple of years ago. It's by this guy named Robert Service. He said, 'A promise made is a debt unpaid, and the trail has its own stern code. . . .'"

As Robert's voice trailed off, I had no problem at all believing that he had, at last, come to the end of that stern trail he had followed so long and faithfully. I felt good that I had been able to bring two special people together. My work had eased the pain not only for Robert Sutherland but also for Martin McElroy's mother. It had taken thirty years, but the mission *was* accomplished.

8

Is There Anything Worse Than Not Knowing?

CAN THERE BE a pain worse than living with the unknown?

Several years ago, a popular science-fiction film called *Blade Runner* asked this question in an unusual manner. Set in the not-too-distant future, the story was about androids, bioengineered creatures that were so much like human beings that only an expert could tell the difference, and then only with the help of a machine that could read reactions of the eyes when certain questions were asked.

There *were* differences, however, between the androids and real human beings. The androids were quicker and more intelligent, and had more stamina. In other words, they evidenced the type of perfection that human beings have never achieved.

Fearing that their creations would one day turn on them, those who manufactured the androids had passed laws to assure that none could live more than a few years and that the most advanced of the androids, the elite warriors used in the outer fringes of the solar system, would never be allowed to set foot on Earth.

Harrison Ford played a police officer who was called out of retirement to hunt down four state-of-the-art androids that had somehow made their way to Earth, determined to find the secret of how to increase the length of their lives.

The police officer quickly found that even such magnificent near-human creatures had a weakness he could exploit: The manufacturers had provided the androids with implanted memories, right down to photographs of their imaginary families.

And even though the highly intelligent warrior androids *knew* that the memories were not real, there was such an overwhelming desire for roots, such a powerful *need*, that at least one of them was willing to risk his safety by trying to recover his precious, though faked, photographs that had been left in his apartment when he had fled.

In a later confrontation with the police officer who was tracking him, that same android angrily described his lack of a past as "an itch that can't be scratched." It was an affecting and disturbing scene, even though the android was not meant to be a sympathetic character.

Blade Runner was a classic film in the science-fiction genre. It dealt with many ethical questions that may actually one day face the human race. To me, however, that one pitiful scene in which the android went back, risking his life, only to find his precious pictures missing, was the most touching, pathetic scene in a movie full of sadness and pathos.

What *does* it feel like to be missing a part of the past? It would have to be like an amputation, when a person continues to feel a missing or "phantom" limb long after it's gone. It raises several questions: Is there anything worse than not knowing? Is bad news better than none at all? Is fantasy more satisfying than harsh knowledge?

Unfortunately, there are real human beings who deal with the question every day of their lives—those who were adopted or abandoned as infants, often cut off from any knowledge of the past by secret court proceedings.

In my capacity as a private investigator, I have come face to face with this form of human anguish more than once. Some cases are harder to forget than others.

~ ~ ~

Dear Norma,

The youngest of five children, I am a thirty-year-old woman who has not seen nor heard from my mother since I was ten. . . .

Twenty years is a long time, I thought, as I began reading that letter. So much can happen in twenty years. Millions of people are born and die over a period of two decades.

Since this young woman had last seen her mother, the entire face of the world had changed dramatically. Communications had become more technological. Plants had been genetically engineered to be resistant to weather. Mikhail Gorbachev had come to power and then lost it. Women had been appointed to the Supreme Court. The Berlin Wall had fallen. And all that time, my would-be client had been looking for her mother.

"My father was very abusive and an alcoholic," the letter continued. "My mother married him when she was sixteen."

Another familiar story. A young girl, perhaps desiring to leave home or madly in love for the first time, takes on more responsibility than she is ready for. She discovers that prince charming is actually the black knight, but by then it's too late to back out. Children have arrived, and the young woman—possibly uneducated—faces severely limited choices in determining the course of her life.

The plight of such a woman was even more difficult twenty years ago than it is today. She could endure the abuse, which would no doubt escalate. She could find someone to take her in and protect her and the children—an unlikely prospect. Or she could do the unthinkable by leaving her children behind.

For the most part, such sad young women exercised the first option. They endured, year after year. Until just recently, with the advent of shelters and the recognition by police and social agencies of the problem's widespread magnitude, many American women were forced to sacrifice their own physical and mental well-being for the good of their children.

Only a small percentage exercised the last option—not nearly as many as one might imagine, considering the sheer number of women in such situations. It speaks well for mothers in general that the overwhelming majority of women will endure almost anything to stay with their children.

To me, a mother who has raised three daughters, the idea of a woman *voluntarily* abandoning her own flesh and blood was totally repugnant. But who knew what kind of horror she had endured? Maybe she had eventually even been murdered by her husband. There were a lot of possibilities, none of them really pleasant.

My first impulse as I read the letter was to turn down the case. I feared there would be only unpleasant news for my prospective client, and I hate to be the bearer of tragic messages. As I read on, however, the sadness of the letter touched me. I knew I would at least have to make an effort.

"I love my mother very much and I miss her every day. Living with the unknown has almost driven me crazy. I have had three nervous breakdowns as a result. My father's mother raised us. My father, who is now deceased, abused us. My grandmother loved us . . . but she couldn't take the place of our mother."

Blinking back tears, I looked over the information the woman named Darlene had sent. Actually, she had provided me with more information than most have when they begin looking for a lost loved one. I had a full name, a date of birth, an old photograph, a last known address, and, perhaps most important, a Social Security number for the missing mother.

In the United States, where people can travel as they please, changing a name is easy. In fact, it's not even illegal unless done for the purpose of defrauding someone. You can change your name as often as you please. And some do it often.

It's not quite as easy to change a Social Security number, especially not today. At one time, it was necessary only to go out to a cemetery, find the tombstone of a deceased child who would have been somewhere near your age, then apply for a birth certificate and Social Security number in that name. Every other necessary document to a new identity could be acquired with those two. Now, however, even children are required to have Social Security numbers. Walk into a modern Social Security office to get a card and you will find yourself explaining why you don't already have one.

Most people who change their names don't go to elaborate lengths. They continue to use their original Social Security number. So if they work or apply for credit, they continue to leave an unbroken paper trail.

The government won't give out information about a person's Social Security number in most cases, but it doesn't matter. Credit bureaus and other agencies have been more than happy to sell files, along with the Social Security numbers, to people who compile computer databases. What the U.S. government won't do, and what the police can't do, private citizens (like me) who subscribe to companies that provide such databases can sometimes easily accomplish.

I dialed up the database on my computer and typed in the Social Security number of the woman known to her children as Barbara. Within moments I had found that the number was still in use—but the name being used was Charlotte, not Barbara. With a little more electronic probing in the ditches along the information highway, I found that the woman now known as Charlotte was married again and living in the southeastern United States. It looked as if there would be a quick resolution of the problem. The only thing needed was verification that Charlotte was really Barbara, the missing mother of five. A call would clear up the matter, and the same computer that had located Charlotte quickly found a telephone number for her.

My hopeful mood didn't last very long. After several unreturned messages on Charlotte's answering machine, I realized I had no choice but to drive to the address I had found and confront the woman in person.

Upon arriving in the small city, I located the correct address and did a little preliminary footwork. There was a possibility that the calls had not been returned because the woman at the other end was not Barbara, the woman whose daughter was so desperate to find her after twenty years. If she wasn't Barbara, though, why was she using Barbara's Social Security number? Had Barbara been murdered? Had someone else assumed her identity?

Employing the tried and true investigatory techniques of my profession, the kind in use long before computers, I began to show Barbara's twenty-year-old picture to the neighbors. Yes, they said, the woman in the old photograph was definitely their neighbor Charlotte.

With some apprehension, I knocked on the door. You never know who will answer or what the reaction will be when you start asking questions. A man in a T-shirt and baggy pants opened the door. I identified myself and asked for Charlotte.

"She ain't home from work yet," he told me. A thin man with tattoos on his forearms, he did not seem surprised that a private detective was asking about his wife. In fact, he seemed rather bored. It was not the kind of reaction I normally get under such circumstances.

"I wonder if you would mind looking at this picture," I asked, "and tell me if it's your wife?"

He glanced at the extended photograph without any visible emotion before answering, "Nope. I ain't never seen that woman before."

"Do you mind if I wait and talk to your wife?" I asked, somewhat puzzled at the turn of events.

"Nope." He shut the door without inviting me in, and without ever having shown any visible curiosity as to why I wanted to find his wife.

I waited in the car until the woman arrived. She was short and stocky. One of Darlene's childhood memories was her mother's "square" feet—short and very wide. Upon seeing Charlotte for the first time, I understood exactly what Darlene meant.

Getting out of my car, I intercepted the woman before she could get to her door. I explained who I was and told her that a young woman was very concerned about the welfare of a mother who had vanished twenty years earlier.

"You've got the wrong person," she told me abruptly in a distinctive husky voice.

"But this picture looks just like you," I said. "You even have a birthmark on your face like the one described to me."

"I don't have any children. I haven't ever been able to have any." She fumbled in her purse, then shoved a driver's license toward me. "Here's *my* identification."

"Your birthdate is the same as Barbara's. And here's Barbara's Social Security number. Does it look familiar?"

"Well," she said grudgingly, "I don't know why that woman is using my Social Security number. But you've got the wrong person. I want you to leave and not come back again."

I showed her Darlene's letter, but I saw she was not going to change her mind. I asked permission to take her picture, then left, almost convinced that I had found the right woman. For whatever reason, emotional denial perhaps, she would not or could not admit her true identity.

I could not bring myself to tell Darlene what had happened, not without being absolutely certain. So I contacted Barbara's sister, Alma, and arranged for her to listen in on a conference call with the woman named Charlotte. Calling on the pretext that I had forgotten to leave a phone number, I let Barbara's sister listen in. Once more, Charlotte strenuously denied being Barbara. She told me that she would have no need for my telephone number because she wouldn't be calling back.

Alma was almost certain that the woman at the other end was her sister. The next day, she made the long drive alone to see Charlotte in person. After the face-to-face meeting—even though the woman known as Charlotte cursed her and ordered her away—Alma was convinced that she had found her long-lost sister.

Alma broke the news to her niece and suggested that it might be better for everyone concerned just to forget Charlotte. But Darlene insisted that she *had* to see for herself. She wanted to meet her mother, to hear her deny who she was. The itch had to be scratched, if Darlene was to keep her sanity.

With Alma and her grandmother (Barbara's mother), Darlene made the long journey with great expectations. Surely when she saw her youngest daughter, the woman would not be able to deny her. If there was some kind of emotional block, surely maternal love would overcome it.

While Darlene and her grandmother waited expectantly in the car, Alma once more knocked at the door. The reaction was instantaneous. The woman called Charlotte stepped out onto the porch and began to curse Alma again. When Barbara's mother recognized her daughter, she also got out of the car to plead with her. But the irate Charlotte continued to deny having any children and screamed that she had never seen the woman who claimed to be her mother. At that point Darlene, who had waited twenty years for the moment, walked over and looked her in the eyes: "Hello, Mother."

"Don't call me your mother!" she told her. "I never saw you before."

Darlene took a step back, almost as if she had been slapped. Then she turned, head down, and walked back to the car. It was a long, sad journey back home for all four of us. But the drama was not quite over.

A week later, Alma's phone rang. At the other end was Charlotte, who was now ready to acknowledge her true identity. She asked Alma to call her youngest child and tell her to come back and see her. Barbara had dropped the charade, the emotional denial, or whatever had caused her to behave the way she did.

Alma hung up and immediately phoned her niece. She broke the news and waited for a shout of joy. The reply was not what Alma expected.

"Let *her* come and see *me*," Darlene said calmly. "I'm not going back there."

My client had accepted the bitter truth of what had happened. She didn't like it much, but she could live with it. Knowing that she and her brothers and sisters had been abandoned deliberately was better than wondering what had happened. That nagging emotional itch that had tormented her, that had even put her in the hospital more than once, had at last been scratched. There would be no reunion, but the healing had begun.

9

Oops! Sorry About That

SOME OF MY colleagues think that simply staying within the law is sufficient as they go about their business. For the most part, they accept no responsibility for the results of their investigations. *Let the buyer beware* is the unspoken thought behind such an attitude. As for me, I don't believe that a thing is necessarily ethical just because it happens to be legal.

Take my specialty, for instance. It has been my experience that *most* people want to be reunited with loved ones from whom they have become separated by circumstance. But the rare case comes across my desk in which the party being sought does not wish to be found. Such cases do not present a dilemma to most investigators. "I work for my clients," one colleague of mine said. "My *only* responsibility is to those clients. I am paid to do investigations. The results of my investigations are turned over to the people who hire me. My job ends there. I'm not a social worker or a missionary."

Investigators with such an attitude may stay strictly within the law, but I see my job as being more than a way to make money; I *am* concerned about the effect I have on those my investigations touch.

After I locate a missing person, I first contact him or her to make sure I have the right party and to ask if he or she is interested in a reunion. Most are overjoyed, but there are those few who want no contact with the past at all.

What do I do then? Because there is no "how to" manual covering every situation relating to this business, I must weigh each case individually. Sometimes I feel there are compelling reasons to give my client the name of a reluctant loved one, but usually I abide by the wishes of the person I have contacted. My principles cost me time and money, but they allow me to sleep at night. A person who *never* suffers for holding on to a principle probably doesn't have any.

Still, despite my best efforts, there are times when things happen that are beyond my control, when a case runs amok. Usually it is because I have not been given all the facts. And then all I can say is, "Oops! Sorry about that," and try to make sure it never happens again.

≈ ≈ ≈

The request for a search came in on one of my standard missing person forms, which can be obtained by mail or by calling my phone service. The form asks for basic information on the client as well as what is known about the person to be located. The form also inquires as to why the client wants to locate the missing party.

On this particular form, the potential client had written, "Lost touch after marriage." The answer seemed vague, so I called the woman who had sent in the form, along with a check. The phone was promptly answered.

"Is this Martha Flynn?" I asked.

"Yes. How may I help you?" she inquired, sounding poised and in control.

"I'm Norma Tillman. I was just reviewing your request that I locate a Mr. Lloyd Franklin. I need a little additional information."

"Certainly. Anything I can do to help. I'd really like to find him. It's been over thirty years since I saw him last."

"How did you know Mr. Franklin?" I asked.

"He lived with our next-door neighbors, the Flints, for a

while. Lloyd and I went to high school together, and then he lived with the Flints one summer."

"Excuse me, but what was the name of the family he lived with? It sounded like you said *Flynn*."

"No, no. Flynn is *my* married name. The *Flints* that lived next door to us. They were the people Lloyd lived with."

"So your relationship to Lloyd Franklin was strictly one of friendship?"

"Yes, we were very close. Just lately I was looking at a high-school yearbook and decided it would be worth the expense to track him down so that we might share some old times."

"Well, you've sent me some good leads," I said, "but you don't have a Social Security number, and there are a lot of people in the world who share the same name. I want you to understand that there could be additional charges if I have to devote an excessive amount of time and expense in this search. Maybe you should set a limit on what you want to spend, just in case."

"That won't be necessary," she said brightly. "Just let me know if I need to send any additional payment."

The information was sketchy, but I had started with less in many cases. I knew Lloyd Franklin's real name, his likely place of birth, the possible year he was born, his brother's name, the name of a woman he had supposedly married, a couple of cities where he might have lived, and the fact that he was a chemist, possibly working for a major corporation.

To those unfamiliar with tracking down people from a cold trail, the above seems like a lot of information. Part of it, however, was "maybe." And even a good investigator can waste a lot of time on "maybes."

I began the search by typing Mr. Franklin's full name and a range of birthdates into my computer. Thanks to advanced technology, it is possible to search with only a first name, a date of birth, or an approximate age. But the narrower the range, such as 1938–39, or 1953–55, or the more specific the information, the shorter the list of possible subjects that comes back.

When you run a name like Smith or Johnson with only a name and range of birthdates, the list is unbelievably long. With less common names, the list is usually reduced to merely frustratingly long. Sometimes you hit paydirt with the first shovelful. Unfortunately, such was not the case with Mr. Franklin. I had hoped that one of the individuals on the first list would match his name perfectly, or even *nearly* so, since my client was a little unsure of details. My next hope was that one of the names would match up either with the city thought to be his place of birth or with one of the cities listed as possible onetime residences.

When these first efforts didn't work, I knew I was probably not going to find Mr. Franklin as quickly as I had hoped. Through the next few days, I continued to run down leads on Lloyd Franklin. A call to the corporation where he had supposedly worked produced a nugget of information.

The director of personnel flatly refused to give me any help at all. When you don't get in the door the first time, you try another tactic. I called the company back. But this time, instead of asking for the director of personnel I asked the receptionist who answered the phone whether there was a published directory of employees. She told me that there was.

"Is it a confidential directory?" I asked.

"No, but it's not mailed out to the public either."

"Let me be honest with you," I said. "I'm a private investigator, and I've been hired to locate a Mr. Lloyd Franklin, who may work for your company or have worked there in the past. He's not in any trouble. He has old friends from his younger days trying to get in contact with him. If you can help me, I promise nobody will know where I got the information."

"Are you sure he's not in some kind of trouble?" I could hear her turning the pages of a book even as we talked. "Because I could get in trouble if he complained."

"He's not in trouble, and your name will never be mentioned," I told her. "*Anybody* with access to that directory could give it out. Nobody will ever know it was you. You have my word."

"All right. I've found a retired account executive by that name. I don't have a current address or phone number, but I can give you his last address while he was with us."

I jotted down the address, then asked one more question.

"I suppose he draws a pension. . . ." I began.

"That *is* confidential information," she quickly told me.

"Thanks for all your help," I said, sincerely. There would be a little more work involved, but I was pretty sure I had the key.

As soon as I hung up the phone, I pulled up Mr. Franklin's old address from another database I use. His name was not listed at that address, but a few quick calls to his former neighbors soon put me on a hot trail. Though none of them had his current address, several said they were sure of the state to which he had moved.

A quick check of vehicle registrations and driver's licenses in that state narrowed my search to a few names. As luck would have it, I scored on the second number.

"Is this Mr. Lloyd Franklin, who once lived with a family by the name of Flint?"

"Yes," he replied, "I once spent a summer with them after my last year of high school. Who is this?"

"Sir, my name is Norma Tillman. I have been hired by a Martha Flynn to find you. It's my practice to get permission before I give out anyone's address and phone number. Would you have any objection to my giving her your phone number and address?"

"Martha, you say?"

"Yes."

"No, I don't mind at all. That was a very good summer for me. It was the year before I went to college."

"In that case, I'll phone her right now."

"How did you find me, Ms. Tillman?"

"We all leave a long paper trail, Mr. Franklin. It would take me a while to explain it all to you."

"I suppose so," he said. "Well, thanks. Tell Martha I'll look forward to hearing from her."

"I'll do that, Mr. Franklin."

Because Mrs. Flynn wasn't home the afternoon that I located Lloyd Franklin, I left a message on her answering machine. It was nearly a week before she returned my call.

"Norma Tillman, please," she said pleasantly when I picked up the phone in my office.

"Yes. How may I help you?"

"This is Martha Flynn. I'm sorry to be so late in returning your call, but I was gone to the Bahamas for a few days."

"I've located Lloyd Franklin, and he says he would be delighted to talk to you."

"So he remembered me, then?"

"Yes. As a matter of fact, he said the summer he spent with the Flints was one of the best of his life."

"Really?"

"That's what he said. I'm glad I could help. I like happy endings. Here's his phone number and current address." I could hear her shuffling paper as she wrote down the information. It was several moments before she spoke again.

"It's going to be happier than you can imagine, Ms. Tillman, especially for my son. He always wanted to meet his biological father, but I didn't feel like I could tell him who he was while my husband was alive. It would have caused a lot of problems. But Elliott is gone now, and I think it's time that my son meets his father."

I was shocked almost beyond words. I had gotten permission from a man to put an old friend in contact with him, and he was about to find out that he had a thirty-year-old son!

"Mrs. Flynn, you deceived me," I said.

"Not really," she responded. "I was afraid you might have some kind of scruples about springing things on Lloyd if you knew the whole story, or that Lloyd wouldn't want to meet his son if he knew, so I just didn't mention the relationship. I figured he would think Martha *Flint* was looking for him. You see, they had a daughter named Martha too.

"I guess you can see now why Lloyd remembers the year he spent with the Flints so fondly. It was mostly because *I* lived next door."

"I feel obligated to call him back . . ." I began.

"Don't bother, Ms. Tillman. I'm going to call him right now. By the way, do I owe you any additional money, or was the check I sent sufficient?"

"It was sufficient," I admitted grudgingly.

For a few minutes after she hung up, I sat quietly. I had mixed emotions about what had just happened. She *had* deceived me, but I had also jumped to conclusions without following up with the right questions. Maybe I would have done the same thing had I been in her place. I just didn't know. I regretted what had happened, but I know that my intentions had been good. There had been no malice intended on my part.

And because you can't squeeze the toothpaste back into the tube, I chalked up the matter to experience, reminding myself to be more careful next time.

I never heard from Lloyd Franklin, so I guess he wasn't too upset. Maybe he was glad. If he called back, though, there was nothing I could have said except, "Oops! Sorry about that."

10

The Case of the Amorous Auto Racer

A WOMAN DOESN'T have to be young and giddy to be taken in by a glamorous man. Even those of us old enough to know that when a thing looks too good to be true, it probably is, sometimes fall victim to what we *wish*, rather than what really is. In other words, romance is alive and well in this country of ours.

If not, how do you explain the huge publishing industry that turns out hundreds of romance novels every year? There is a category for practically every taste in the world—everything from sweet period pieces set in rural America to sultry adventures among dusky natives and swaying palm trees. Finding that one true love is a tradition as old as Western civilization. Even in a time of arranged marriages, popular literature and drama extolled the glamour of romantic encounters under a full moon. Is it any wonder that *Romeo and Juliet* is still as popular today as it was when Shakespeare penned it? Even many independent, career-oriented women—whether they admit it or not—want to meet Mr. Right.

A woman cannot have been raised in the Western world without being exposed to the glamour of romantic love and star-struck lovers. It's hard not to buy into it, at least occasionally. Things being the way they are, I wasn't surprised when a childhood friend of mine began to talk about her latest romantic interest with as much enthusiasm as she had used to describe her *first* boyfriend when we were in junior high school.

"You'll have to see him to believe, Norma. That's all I can say. If a television scriptwriter sat down and dreamed up the perfect man, he would be just like Phillip."

It was easy to remember Penny as an adolescent girl in love for the first time. To me, she hadn't changed a lot since school. Oh, she has a few lines here and there, but who doesn't? Her hair is still a warm auburn and her complexion has held up well through the years.

Even as a teenager, Penny was never what you would call flighty or frivolous. It was pretty easy to see that this Phillip, whoever he was, had pretty much swept her off her feet.

"He sounds almost too good to be true," I said. Too often in my career, it has been my sad duty to show Cinderella that her prince charming doesn't look as good close-up as he appeared at first glance. In fact, more often than not, he has rust on his sword and moth holes in his velvet shirt.

"Now don't start up with that, Norma!" Penny said, only partly in jest. "Just because you run across shady characters in your job, that doesn't mean *all* men are scoundrels."

"No," I replied, "but there are enough scoundrels to support a lot of private investigators."

"Well, I can tell you that Phillip Loveday is *not* a scoundrel." She looked at me in a way that said she very much wanted to be right about him and that she could use a little moral support.

"All right," I smiled. "Tell me all about Phillip."

"Well, first of all, he's handsome. Not in a pretty way like Robert Redford." She paused for a moment, as if looking at a menu in her head. "Phillip is more like Clint Eastwood or James Garner. You know, good-looking, but *rugged*.

"Here, see for yourself." She handed me a Polaroid of a silver-haired man, and I had to admit that he was indeed handsome, even by Hollywood standards (though not as handsome as my favorite, Kevin Costner).

"So what does your prince charming do for a living?" I asked, sipping my iced tea.

"He's a race-car driver. I was at the airport waiting for a friend, and he came in and sat down next to me in the restaurant."

"He picked you up in an airport restaurant?" That scenario *did* surprise me.

"Oh, it wasn't like *that*. After all, I'm not a child anymore, and neither is Phillip. He's a widower with two grown sons—he even has grandchildren."

"All right, he's a grandfather, and he's a race-car driver. Go on."

"Well, auto racing is really more of a hobby than anything else," Penny said. "He doesn't *have* to work at all because he inherited money from his parents."

"Oh, and how much money does he have?"

"Norma, how would I know that? I know he has money because he owns about six classic cars in mint condition. In fact, he's got a black 1963 Corvette for sale right now."

"Where does he live?" I asked carefully. Little warning bells were going off in my head. This guy definitely sounded too good to be true, and I didn't want my friend to be hurt if she found out that instead of living on a private estate with a fleet of expensive cars, he lived in an efficiency apartment somewhere, paid outrageous alimony, and drove a beat-up car—or worse.

Penny named a small Louisiana town not too far from New Orleans. It just happened that I had some business in New Orleans at that time.

"Look, Penny, I'm going to be in New Orleans in a few days. Why don't I just—?"

"Don't you even *think* about it!" she interrupted. "I'm not going to ruin my relationship with Phillip by having a private detective spying on him."

"I wouldn't be acting as a private detective," I told her. "I'd be acting as a friend who wants the very best for you."

"Absolutely not!" she insisted. "The discussion is closed. I'm *not* going to give you enough information to dig into his private affairs."

"Okay. Forget I mentioned it."

She waited a moment to see whether I intended to ask any more questions, then smiled when none were forthcoming. I didn't need any more information. I had Phillip's name and the town where he allegedly lived. I knew it wouldn't be hard to check him out.

I have found a lot of people with far less information than Penny had given me during the course of a conversation. After all, I *am* a good detective. Some people have even accused me of having psychic powers. But I wouldn't need them to find Phillip Loveday—not if he lived where he had told Penny. And not if his name was really Phillip Loveday.

After arriving in the Louisiana town Penny had mentioned, it didn't take me long to find the address that had come up when I ran Phillip Loveday through a couple of my computer databases.

To say that the address was an exclusive development would be an understatement. The entire cluster of expensive homes, built along a private airstrip no less, was nestled behind a high brick wall and guarded by a huge wrought-iron gate.

For a moment I was a little envious. I still had my suspicions, however. For all I knew, Phillip might well have been a grease monkey working for one of the families that lived inside the pala-tial housing development.

The gate was locked, but it didn't take me long to figure out the system. It was set up like an apartment building. There was a button under each house number, but there were no names. I had Phillip's number, but I didn't want to make him suspicious if he was there. I pushed the button for another residence. It was answered in a moment by a female, who sounded very young.

"Yes?" the voice inquired.

"I'm visiting at the Loveday house, and their phone is busy. Would you mind buzzing me in?"

"Where are you visiting?" came the reply.

"At the Loveday house." I held my breath for a moment. Then the huge metal gates swung open. As I drove through, some sort of sensing device closed the gates behind me.

Phillip Loveday's house was like something out of *Lifestyles of the Rich and Famous*: three stories high, with a huge swimming pool visible in the back and a lawn that looked as if it had been manicured with scissors. I took a deep breath and rang the door-bell. A moment later a pretty, freckled woman opened the door. She was young, and she carried a toddler on her hip. I remem-bered what Penny had told me about Phillip's grandchildren. *She could be his daughter*, I thought.

"May I help you?" she asked.

"Is this Phillip Loveday's house?"

"Yes, but he isn't here. He's in Houston for a race." She stared at me with a question in her eyes.

"I'm here to look at the car that's for sale." A good investiga-tor always has a cover story ready. I handed her one of my busi-ness cards. *Well*, I thought, *You were wrong about this one, Norma. Phillip seems to be checking out.*

I was happy for Penny.

"Oh, the Corvette." She glanced at my card. "All right. Come inside, and we'll go out the back way to the garage. By the way, I'm Joan, and this is Tammy," she indicated the child on her hip, "and that's Michael." Michael was about three, with close-cropped blond hair and an impish grin.

Once again, I breathed a sigh of relief that my suspicions had been wrong. Penny would be angry when she found out what I had done. But she could always tell Phillip that I was a sports car enthusiast (who also just happened to be a private investigator) who had stopped in for a look at his Corvette on my way to New Orleans.

As we walked through the spacious living room, I glanced at several photographs sitting on the piano and saw a studio portrait of the two children with the man in the Polaroid picture Penny had shown me.

In the huge back yard, a miniature railroad track circled around inside a white fence. The red-and-black miniature locomotive parked by the porch was just the right size for children. Phillip Loveday was obviously a doting grandfather.

"Do you mind if I shoot a few pictures of the car?" I asked as we approached the garage.

"Be my guest," the young woman said.

Walking around the car, I discreetly shot pictures of the woman and the two little girls, as well as the house and swimming pool. Maybe Penny would go easy on me when I showed her pictures of the estate and Phillip's grandchildren.

A few minutes later we stood at the front door, ready to part company.

"Do the kids like to go driving with their grandfather?" I asked.

"Their grandfather?" The young woman seemed puzzled. "Oh," she said, smiling. "Phillip isn't their grandfather. He's their father."

For a moment I was at a loss for words. I had been so happy for Penny that I had accepted what appeared obvious rather than asking the right questions.

Jumping to conclusions is a bad practice for an investigator.

"Don't be embarrassed." The young woman seemed genuinely concerned about my discomfort. "A lot of people make the same mistake. I'm Phillip's third wife, and Tammy is his tenth child."

I apologized and removed my foot from my mouth. Not only would I be taking bad news to Penny, but there also wasn't even a silver cloud on the horizon.

~ ~ ~

"Hello," Penny said.

"This is Norma." I waited to see whether she would hang up on me.

"Where are you?" she asked.

"I'm in New Orleans." I waited a few moments, then plunged in. "I stopped off and visited Phillip's place earlier today."

"I know. He apparently checked in with his wife right after you left. Then he called *me* with some cock-and-bull story about how the woman you talked to was his ex-wife and she just needed a place to live for a while."

"Do you believe him?" I asked.

"Of course not."

"Are you mad at me?"

"Yes, but I'll get over it. You were right. There are a lot of scoundrels out there, and Phillip just happened to be one of them. I know that you did the best you knew how for me. I'll survive this. I've survived worse."

"Well, keep in mind what *I* said, but don't forget what *you* said. There really are some good men out there. You just have to watch out for the bad ones."

"Did you get good pictures of Phillip's wife while you were photographing the car?"

"I think so. How did you know?"

"Phillip was very upset about the pictures you snapped."

"Should I throw them away?"

"No, I'd like to get a look at my competition—even though I told him never to show his face around here again."

"Good for you," I said.

"One more thing, Norma."

"What's that?"

"The next time I'm having such a great dream, let me sleep just a little bit longer."

11

She Couldn't Win for Losing

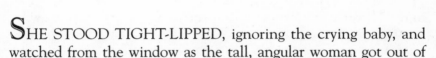

SHE STOOD TIGHT-LIPPED, ignoring the crying baby, and watched from the window as the tall, angular woman got out of her car, then removed a portable bassinet.

"I don't understand why you're doing this," her husband said, picking up the screaming infant and cradling her on his shoulder. There was sadness in his voice. "Little Susan is everything I expected."

"Well," the woman snapped, "if you had to be here all day and listen to her constant crying, you wouldn't think she was so perfect." She folded her arms across her chest and grimly watched the woman from the adoption agency carry the bassinet up the walk.

It had seemed simple enough when the advertisement ran in the paper just before Christmas, with pictures of numerous infants. YOU CAN HAVE A BABY FOR CHRISTMAS, the headline read.

Much later, the woman who ran a home for children would become notorious as an alleged broker of black-market babies. In the 1940s, however, at the time of the ad, she was touted as a great humanitarian.

John and Lyda had called the children's home. "We'd like to try out one of those babies you advertised in the paper," Lyda had told the baby broker.

Shortly afterward, the woman from the home had shown up with baby Susan in a wicker bassinet. John had been deliriously happy with his new daughter. And why not? Lyda thought. *He* was the one who wanted a baby in the first place. And *he* didn't have to listen to all that crying or change dirty diapers all day long.

Wearily the man walked over and opened the door. "Come in," he said to the woman standing on the porch.

"Well, I have your new baby," she said, maneuvering the bassinet through the door. "I hope you haven't been inconvenienced too much."

"I like Susan well enough," the man said, "but she cries a lot...."

"You don't have to explain a thing to me," the woman told him. "The important thing is that you're happy with your baby."

Without further ado, the woman bent over and lifted a dark-haired infant from the bassinet. "This is baby Ellen," she said, handing the baby to Lyda. "Try *her* for a while. I hope she's more to your satisfaction."

Briskly, and without further delay, the woman took Susan from the man and tucked her into the same bassinet she had used to transport the new baby. After she had gone, John walked over and pushed the blanket away.

"She's pretty," he said. "As pretty as Susan."

"You think *all* babies are pretty," Lyda said, holding Ellen stiffly in her arms. The baby, perhaps sensing the woman's animosity, began to cry.

"*See*, there's no relief for me. You'll be gone all day while I'm stuck here with somebody else's baby."

"She's *your* baby now," the man chided softly.

"I guess we'll see about that," Lyda snapped.

A few days later, Lyda called the home once again. "Come and get this baby," she said. "I don't like it any better than the last one."

Nobody ever showed up the second time, though. Apparently the customer got only two chances at picking a winner.

≈ ≈ ≈

I sat stunned as my new client unfolded the story in my office. I had read quite a bit about the alleged baby broker, and there had even been a made-for-television movie about her life. But I still found it hard to believe that anyone could be so cold toward a helpless baby.

To sit in the presence of a human being who had been treated like a mongrel puppy was disturbing, to say the least. To hear that very same person calmly discuss the matter rattled me even more.

"How did she treat you?" I asked.

"She hated me," Ellen said. "So she treated me the way you treat someone you hate." A tired woman, Ellen looked as if she had just about endured all she could stand.

"Some people just can't relate to children," I said. "That's why the screening process is so arduous today. Maybe she didn't hate you. Maybe she just had trouble relating to all children."

"No, she *hated* me! There's no other word to explain the way she abused me all my life." Ellen's face colored as she spoke.

"Every day, beginning with my earliest memories, she called me ugly and stupid. She would get right down in my face and ask, 'Do you know how stupid you are? Have I told you lately how ugly you are?' And it wasn't once in a while, like when she was upset. It was her consuming passion to let me know just how contemptible she thought I was. She made it perfectly clear—she wished I'd never been born"

"What about your father?" I asked. "Where was he when this was going on?"

"He was at work most of the time. She didn't mistreat me in front of him. The only peaceful times I had were when he was home. He really loved me," Ellen said, a genuine smile of affection crossing her face.

"I used to dream that one day Daddy would throw her out and come home with a new wife, someone who would be kind to me. Once, when I was about five, I even suggested it.

"He just smiled sadly and told me that he had a responsibility to carry the cross he had voluntarily picked up. Whatever was really wrong with their relationship, he pretty well shielded me from it.

"Of course, she was always telling me that *I* was the problem. She told me that everything had been fine until I was delivered to their door. I got enough to eat and had clothes on my back, but that woman never gave me a moment of love.

"My father died while I was still in high school, and after that I received the full brunt of her rage twenty-four hours a day. As soon as I graduated, I got away from her."

"Well, nobody could blame you for that," I said. "Did she keep in touch through the years?"

"I kept in touch with her, but she barely responded. Even when my children were born, there was never a card or a birthday or Christmas gift from her. It was like we didn't exist. Unfortunately, that changed just a couple of years before she died."

"How did it change?" I asked, thoroughly caught up in the story of a woman as callous and cruel as any I had ever heard of.

"She became too ill to take care of herself. Then she called and asked me to move her into my house so I could cook for her and take care of her."

"That's unbelievable!" I blurted.

"I know. She had money of her own, so I suggested that she hire a nurse or move into one of those assisted-living places. But she cried and said she wanted to be near her little girl during her last days on earth."

"You didn't believe her, did you?"

"Not really, but I guess I hoped she had seen her past mistakes and would try to make amends for it—maybe even come to treat my children as her grandchildren."

"Did she?"

"No. She was even worse than she had been when I was a child. The kinder I tried to be, the more vicious she became.

"Being the kind of person she was, my mother tried to hold my inheritance over my head. She talked about how much money I would inherit when she died, but she wouldn't even help pay the grocery bill. She never offered me a penny.

"Finally, it all came to a head on a day when one of my mother's nieces was visiting. My mother went on and on about how badly I was treating her. When her niece had the gall to accuse me of not being a good daughter . . . well, I just blew up.

"I told my cousin that I wanted her *and* my mother out of my house. She took her without any argument. Looking back, it seems likely that my mother had promised her the same thing she had been trying to blackmail me with—money.

"The niece, though, apparently had enough sense to get it in writing. My mother signed a power of attorney, and the niece took over her finances."

Ellen paused for a moment as if embarrassed by what she was about to say, as if she wanted to make certain that I did not misinterpret her motives.

"When my mother died without a will, that niece had a judge declare her the legal heir. I tried to contest because I was her adopted daughter, but . . ."

"But what?" I asked.

"I can't find the paperwork about my adoption. If I can prove I was legally adopted, I stand to inherit a lot of money, and I think I deserve *something* for all the abuse I suffered through the years at my mother's hands!"

"So do I," I told Ellen. "So do I."

Investigations almost always hold surprises. Sometimes when I start out with a lot of information, I hit a roadblock early on. At other times, I have so little information that I almost expect to fail, and things move right along.

In Ellen's case, I knew the place to start looking was the city where she was adopted. Despite the later allegations that babies had been bought and sold for years at the infamous children's home, the appearance of respectability had always been maintained. That meant records of a sort did exist.

Once I located court records and matched up dates, Ellen's life story, prior to her adoption, unfolded. By the time I reached the end of the trail, I was more shaken than ever by her story.

Ellen's biological mother had been a teenager, possibly a victim of incest, who was committed to a mental institution while in the seventh month of her pregnancy. Her baby was born in the institution and was allowed to stay there for several months—until her mother got involved in a fight with another patient. Then baby Ellen had been removed for her own safety. That was when she ended up in her adoptive home.

How heavily can the deck be stacked against one person? I asked myself as one ugly fact after another emerged.

Ellen's was a horror story, like something from a Stephen King novel—the child of an incestuous relationship, born inside a mental institution, falls into the hands of a woman who is alleged to be the most flagrant seller of babies in this century and is then placed with a sociopathic woman who abuses her unmercifully. In a novel, of course, the story would have to be toned down. Nobody would believe that such a thing could really happen in the twentieth century.

The paper trail ended at the point where Ellen was put up for adoption. The records were sealed, so, armed with dates and names, I went to the state where Ellen had been taken when she was adopted. After searching through stacks of dusty records, however, I came up empty. I could find absolutely no record that any paperwork had been filed with that state.

Shortly afterward, Ellen's attorney obtained a court order to open her sealed adoption records. Then I hand carried the order to the state's Department of Human Services. Ellen and I were both nervous that day—I because I didn't want to see my client suffer any additional pain, she because a substantial sum of money was riding on the contents. I'm sorry to report that fate was not finished with Ellen.

We learned that her adoption had never been finalized. Ellen's file contained the letter from the adoptive mother asking the agency to come get the baby, but no indication of any response from the agency—and certainly no completed adoption certificate. In the eyes of the law, there had never been an adoption—even though my client had a sealed adoption record in her name.

I had done all I could. But that shadowy creature called justice is sometimes hard to pin down. Is there any doubt that Ellen was morally entitled to the money that a loving adoptive father had earned? Or that Ellen deserved payment for the abuse at the hands of an angry, vicious child abuser? I think not.

Unfortunately, judges and courts operate not according to moral entitlement but according to evidence. The entire fortune went to the niece. Ellen got nothing except the hateful memory of a woman who had managed to humiliate her one final time—from the grave. We have an old saying that seems to apply to Ellen with a vengeance: *She couldn't win for losing.*

12

Sometimes You Wade in Deep Water

UNDER THE TRENCH COAT, there's always a gun, right? Not necessarily.

It's true that Richard Diamond and Nick Charles and even Spenser—practically all the private eyes in movies, television, and detective fiction—always seem to have a pistol tucked away, ready for quick use. And it's also true that some real-life investigators regularly carry weapons. Those who provide security and bodyguard services would be foolish to go unarmed. That a client is in need of such services implies that danger exists.

In my opinion and experience, however, most private investigators—most of the time—have little use for a handgun. The main investigative tool is between the ears. With an active, fertile brain, a pad and pencil, a camera, a tape recorder, and—these days—a computer, most investigators are completely equipped for business.

An alert investigator, however, is never lulled into believing that delving into the lives of other people is entirely safe. After all, no one hires a private detective unless he or she has something to lose. People who are perfectly happy rarely have need of an investigator, and people who turn over rocks for a living must expect occasionally to encounter something slimy. So it's best to remain alert, even when things look perfectly normal. It never fails—when I least expect it, the unexpected happens!

"Mrs. Tarpin, I'm absolutely certain that you can find a private detective back home. Frankly, I don't understand why you've come all the way to Nashville to try and hire me."

"My lawyer recommended you. He says that you're good at what you do, and that you're honest. I can't take a chance on hiring a private investigator who might try to sell his services to my husband for more money."

Lois Tarpin was in her early forties, with hair that was a deep chestnut color. An elegant woman, she obviously had the money to hold the ravages of time at bay. The clothes she was wearing had never hung on a rack at Sears or J.C. Penney. In fact, they had probably never hung on a rack at all. Every item, from the expensive loafers to her embroidered vest, looked as if it had been made just for her.

"Most private investigators are honest people just trying to earn a living, Mrs. Tarpin." There are always those few in the business of private investigations—as in any business—who leave such bad impressions that we all suffer.

"I don't doubt that," she said. "But my husband has more money than you would imagine. He's a powerful, high-profile man. Everybody in the city knows him. I'm just afraid the temptation would be too much for most people—or even that an investigator might boast to his friends that he was investigating my husband.

"I need the goods on him before he even *suspects* that I plan to divorce him."

"Just exactly what do you expect me to find—*if* I decide to take the job?" I asked.

"I am almost certain that he's having an affair with the manager of his hotel."

"Why do you suspect that?" I asked, wondering what kind of hotel could be so profitable.

When she told me the name of the establishment, I suddenly understood. It was a place that tourists visit in droves—when they can get reservations. Just having slept and eaten there gives a tourist a certain status.

"The usual reasons. He's working late. He attends one civic affair after another, and I'm invited less and less often. He keeps a suite empty now at all times so he'll have a place to sleep when he's just *too tired* to drive all the way home—a ten-minute drive, mind you. We don't even *sleep* together more than once a month these days. Don't even ask about our sex life."

It wasn't exactly a new story. In fact, it was one I had heard often in my career.

"Do you understand, Mrs. Tarpin, that it's going to be very expensive to have me leave Nashville for an undetermined length of time? I have files stacked up now that need my immediate attention."

What I didn't say was that many of those cases I specialize in, involving people who are trying to find lost loved ones, are often brought to me by people who can't always pay well. Sometimes— if the price is right—I take other jobs so I can work on those that are so dear to me. Divorce work, however, is at the bottom of my list of favorites, and I seldom take it.

"I understand completely. My lawyer explained how expensive a good private investigator can be." She opened her purse and slid a cashier's check across the desk. It was made out to me, and the amount almost took my breath away. "Here's a retainer. When it's used up, let me know, and I'll have another one ready."

"All right, Mrs. Tarpin. It's your money." I reached into a drawer and brought out my pad and pen. "I'll need to know everything you can tell me about your husband. Don't hold back anything. I never know what's going to be useful until I get out in the field."

My first stop in the city, after getting a centrally located motel room, was the main branch of the public library. It was a fairly good research facility. Microfiche newspaper files pretty well confirmed what Mrs. Tarpin had told me. Her father had originally owned the hotel, but her husband, George Tarpin, had been in control since long before the death of her father.

When I had finished my research at the library, however, there was already a nagging suspicion in the back of my mind that things were not quite as they appeared to be.

The first mention of George Tarpin in the local newspapers was thirty years old. He had been a minor labor union official who later went into the trucking business. That old story dealt with unproved allegations that union officials had pressured certain companies to do business with Tarpin. But the matter had apparently ended there.

Since then, Tarpin had gotten nothing but rave reviews from the local press. The most recent newspaper photographs showed a handsome, silver-haired man of perhaps fifty cutting the ribbon at a public building. He was involved, it seemed, in every charity imaginable and sat on half a dozen prominent boards. He didn't seem to be anything like the selfish, cheating man his wife had described to me. He appeared as public figures so often do, as a pillar of the community. But I had been in the business too long to completely trust either newspaper accolades or the descriptions of an estranged press. Time and good detective work would tell the real story.

∽ ∽ ∽

I almost missed the man I was tailing an hour into the stakeout. I had been focused on his maroon Jaguar, parked in its reserved spot in front of the hotel, when an unmarked white van pulled from the garage. George Tarpin was sitting on the passenger side.

Fortunately, the female driver caught a red light, and I was able to fall in behind them in my rental car. I almost lost them two more times. I was not prepared when the van stopped in front of an office building, where George Tarpin stepped down and briskly walked through the front door. He was carrying a large leather briefcase.

Before I could find a place to pull over, Tarpin was back in the van. I lingered at the next light and let them pass me. The van made two more stops within ten minutes, one at a small grocery and deli, the other at a tobacco shop.

Between stops, the driver of the van seemed to be making unnecessary turns and double-backs, though I couldn't be sure because I was in a city unfamiliar to me. I was positive I wouldn't be able to tail Tarpin successfully after dark, not if he drove like the young woman behind the wheel of the van. So I decided that a tracking device was in order for his car.

Three hours and perhaps twenty stops later, the van returned to the hotel. I coasted by as Tarpin was dropped at the door. The woman behind the wheel was older than she had looked from a distance, perhaps thirty. She was dressed with too much class, at least in my opinion, to be a professional van driver. I wondered whether she was the woman who had aroused Mrs. Tarpin's suspicions as her husband's possible mistress. If so, there had been no hint of romance visible while I was behind them.

I found a parking space less than a hundred yards away. A few minutes later, I dropped my car keys beside the luxury car. Getting down on my knees, I made a big production of fishing around for them. By the time I got up, casually dusting myself off, there was a tracking device attached to the underside of the Jaguar. I looked at my watch and decided to take a chance that my man wouldn't leave again for a couple of hours. I needed to freshen up and get something to eat.

For the next two days, George Tarpin drove straight to work, then straight home after leaving the hotel—not the typical behavior of a philandering husband. Of course, he and the woman suspected of being his mistress could have been doing anything in his private suite without my being any the wiser.

The woman's name, I learned, was Eileen Springer, and she was indeed the hotel's general manager. Her picture was on display behind the counter, right beside George Tarpin's and just below that of my client's father, the deceased founder of the hotel. I had seen it when I went inside to use the restroom.

By the evening of the third day, I seemed to be getting nowhere quickly, and I was ready to try a different tactic. The possibility of hiring in as a hotel employee crossed my mind a couple of times, but it didn't really seem feasible. To gain enough trust for serious snooping would have consumed more time than I was willing to spend.

Then, as almost always happens on a stakeout when it seems that nothing is ever going to happen, my man strode out the front door and lowered himself into his car. He looked around before getting in, his gaze passing over me. I had traded in the rental car for an equally inexpensive but different model, and this time I was wearing a blond wig—just in case Tarpin was more alert than most people. He did seem a little nervous, although he gave no sign of recognizing me.

The Jaguar was a block away when I pulled from the curb. At the end of the second block, my quarry made an abrupt left-hand turn across traffic without signaling. Oncoming drivers blew their horns in outrage. Unable to make the turn after him, I proceeded to the next intersection and headed in the same direction, parallel to Tarpin.

My tracking device was beeping at the same intensity, so I knew he wasn't far away. At the next intersection I turned right and was behind him again, several cars back. This time I was ready when he made another abrupt left-hand turn. Once more I drove to the next block and turned left again.

By this time there was no doubt in my that mind that George Tarpin was watching for a tail. Intelligence operatives, both in government and in private security, are taught that if a car stays with them through three abrupt turns, especially against traffic, they are probably being tailed. Because I knew the same techniques, I didn't stay behind him. I had the tracking device as insurance, just in case I made a wrong guess. After making the next right turn, I was three cars back from him.

Tarpin made similar maneuvers twice more before hitting the interstate. My tracking unit enabled me to stay with him, but well out of sight. In the gathering darkness, all he could see were headlights anyway. When he took an exit near a suburban shopping mall, my little stalker machine was still beeping contentedly.

The traffic was extremely heavy on the mall parking lot, which was probably why it had been chosen for a meeting place. There was little chance that anyone would notice one more luxury car, much less remember it. George Tarpin pulled in two spaces away from a long black Cadillac with darkened windows. I drove past, as if looking for a parking space, so I could obtain the tag number to identify the occupants. A chill went up my spine as the front passenger door of the Cadillac opened. A husky man with a shiny suit and shiny hair—like a character from the original *Godfather* movie—got out and circled around to the rear driver's side door. At the same time, Tarpin was popping his trunk and walking around to the back of his Jaguar. The driver of the Cadillac also got out and stood in front of his car, surveying the area. One hand hovered near his belt in an expectant manner.

Making my second pass, I looked him directly in the eye. For a moment, I thought he was staring at me, that he had "made me," as we say in the business. It was like looking into the eyes of a lizard. My first impulse was to floor the accelerator and get as far away as possible. I fought the inclination. Such an action would have brought exactly the kind of attention I didn't need.

George Tarpin approached the Cadillac, carrying the same bulging briefcase he had carried on his rounds in the van. The first man opened the car door for him but did not stop scanning the area with his eyes. His hand was always near his waistband.

There was a possibility, I suppose, that the man I was following was meeting with the mayor and his staff. There was a possibility that he was conducting a quick board meeting for one of his many charities. I didn't believe either possibility for a minute. I learned long ago that the most obvious explanation is almost always the right one.

I had watched Tarpin making some kind of collection two days earlier, no doubt about that. That he and the person or persons in the Cadillac were splitting up the collection and working out business details seemed equally probable to me. And I had no doubt whatsoever that there would be serious repercussions for anybody caught doing surveillance work in the vicinity.

Five rows away, I pulled my car into a slot and sat trembling. What had I been lulled into? Whatever it was, I knew I was in over my head. I had no intention of driving by that Cadillac or of tailing George Tarpin again, although I did note the tag number when the black vehicle drove by on its way out of the mall lot.

When I got back to my motel room, I was still trembling, partly from fear and partly from rage. My client would have some explaining to do.

"I think it's about time you told me what's *really* going on," I told Lois Tarpin, making absolutely no effort to be smiling and polite. We were at a restaurant in another suburban mall. After what had happened, I didn't even want her to know where my motel was. And I certainly didn't want to go to her house.

"What's *really* going on is that I want a divorce. I had hoped you would come up with the evidence to make it possible," she snapped.

"Did it occur to you that I might get into serious trouble tailing your husband while he was meeting with his associates—whoever and whatever they are? I'm betting they don't represent the YMCA or the Boy Scouts of America."

"No, your first impression was right. My husband is some kind of mob kingpin. He doesn't discuss business with me, but I'm pretty perceptive. I figured out a long time ago where the real money comes from."

"Why didn't you just tell me?"

"The bookkeeper, one of my father's original employees, questioned inconsistencies in certain accounts at the hotel two years

ago. A week later he was dead. The police report said it was an accident, that his brakes were bad. I don't know. What I *do* know is that
the brakes on Wiley's car had just been fixed a few days earlier."

"All the more reason that you should have told me," I said
through tight lips.

"Would you have taken the case?"

"No, I wouldn't have."

"He would have spotted a male detective right away, no matter how careful the detective was," Lois Tarpin said. "George is
paranoid. He thinks everyone, from the FBI to the IRS, has him
under surveillance. But I knew he'd never suspect a woman. He
thinks we're all stupid. Besides, my lawyer said you were good."

"If I wasn't good, I might very well be dead right now. For the
sake of argument, just suppose I *had* gotten the goods on him and
his girlfriend. What makes you think a man like him would even
care about being accused of adultery when he's involved with
who knows what?"

"Because his image is the most important thing in the world
to him. George has always been ashamed of his childhood. He
was raised in the slums; now he plays golf with the mayor and the
governor and sometimes congressmen. Once he even played with
a former president. George is also a big contributor to our church.
It's important to him that the whole world see him as a straight-
up family man."

"Well, it goes without saying that I'm off the case. I'll give
back all your money except for three days, plus expenses."

"No, that won't be necessary," she said. "George has ten times
the amount I gave you stuffed in his car's glove compartment,
behind the horn button, and under the spare tire—just in case he
needs to get away fast. He gives me more money than I know
what to do with—he can't put it in the bank. There's over five
hundred thousand dollars in the floor safe in our bedroom. So just
keep what I paid you for all your trouble."

"Have you thought about going to the authorities?" I asked.

"I don't know who to trust. With evidence of adultery to hold over his head, he might have let me out just to keep it hushed up. If I talked to the wrong cop, I'd be dead."

"Tell you what," I offered. "I think I know a couple of honest police officers in this city. I've worked with them before. Why don't I get in touch with one of them before I leave? Not all cops are on the take."

"I know that," she said, tears welling in the corners of her eyes. "But how do you tell them apart before it's too late?"

The next day, the detective put down the phone, pursed his lips, and shook his head ruefully. He had just run the tag number of the black Cadillac.

"Norma, take my advice. Pack your bags and get the heck out of Dodge. You've waded in over your head. I may very well have to make up some reason for my superior as to why I just ran that tag through the computer."

"Who did it come back to?" I asked.

"You don't want to know," he told me.

"I trust you, you're an honest cop. Isn't there something you can do about George Tarpin?"

"Not and survive. It's like your client told you. Not all cops are on the take, but you can't always separate the good guys from the bad guys in time to protect yourself.

"Most of the big shots who look out for guys like Tarpin don't know what they're *really* sponsoring. What's more, they don't want to know. Organized crime buys a lot of politicians with campaign contributions and charity donations. If the president had as good a public-relations staff as most gangsters, he'd be a shoo-in for the next election."

He leaned back in his chair and surveyed me through narrowed eyes. "Like I said, I suggest you leave town and forget everything you saw and heard. Now, if you'll excuse me, I'm going to try and think up a reasonable explanation for checking on a vehicle belonging to a man who regularly eats breakfast at the governor's mansion."

I took the officer's advice and left town. I would have done something for Mrs. Tarpin if it had been within my power. But I'm just a small-town private investigator, not a special agent trained by the FBI. Sometimes a person can wade in deep water without realizing it. But once you know you're in over your head, the only way to survive is to swim for shore.

13

Back from the Dead

HOLLYWOOD HAS PRODUCED many movies about people given up for dead who suddenly reappear—from a war zone, a desert island, or even another dimension or time. Sometimes the resurrection theme has been treated as high drama, as seems fitting to me; at other times it has been used as a platform for humor.

In real life, such events are relatively rare, at least in technologically advanced countries. Expanding communications and advanced methods of record-keeping have shrunk the world to the size of a global village and made it harder for people to disappear without a trace.

Despite all the advances, though, I was confronted with a "back from the dead" case not too very long ago. In fact, it became my duty to be the reluctant and unwitting bearer of such startling news.

It all began when I received a completed questionnaire for my computer database, the Reunion Network. (With this growing database, I can match two people who want to find each other, anywhere in the world.) Accompanying the form was a letter in which the following words jumped off the page at me: "I haven't seen my daughter in forty years. I was awarded custody, but her father took her from me and I never saw her again. . . ."

A plea from a mother to find a lost child is one I've always found difficult to pass up. I immediately called my correspondent to collect the details I would need in my search. The phone was answered immediately, as if the woman at the other end had been waiting.

"Hello."

"This is Norma Tillman. I need to speak with Elizabeth Kuhn."

"Norma Tillman?" The woman sounded puzzled. Then, as if a light had come on, she realized who I was. "Norma Tillman, the private investigator I saw on television! Did you receive the questionnaire I filled in?"

"Yes, I have it in front of me. Why don't you tell me the complete story and we'll see what I can do to help you?"

"Where should I start?"

"With the circumstances of your daughter's disappearance. I'll also need all the information you can give me about her and her father, including his Social Security number, occupation, hobbies, and last known address. Before we get to the details, though, why don't you just kind of give me an overview of the entire story."

"Well, we had three children. Pamela was the youngest, always his favorite. He'd pick all three of the children up once a month—unless Pam was sick, then he wouldn't come at all. Six months after the divorce, he asked if Pamela could come and spend a few weeks with him. There didn't seem to be any harm in it. She wasn't in school yet—only five years old—and he had always brought her back on time."

"Elizabeth, was your husband violent? Did he ever do anything to the children?" I gently probed.

"No!" She sounded shocked. "I wouldn't have let him take them for visits if that had been the case."

"Don't get upset. I have to know these things."

"Well, that wasn't the case with my husband. He was a pathological liar and an alcoholic, but he wouldn't have hurt his children."

"Exactly why did you divorce him?" I asked.

"Like I told you, he was a liar!" she snapped. "And he was always running around with other women." It was obvious that she was still angry after forty years.

"What kind of work did your ex-husband do?"

"He was a salesman, and let me tell you, that man could sell snow in the Arctic. Sometimes he'd make huge amounts of money and then sit around for weeks. Then he'd get out one of those sales magazines or answer an ad in the paper and work for a few more weeks. I always knew that if he ever got into some kind of sales that really interested him, he'd become a millionaire. But it didn't happen when I was married to him."

"How did you first learn that he had taken Pamela?"

"When I called and the telephone company told me the phone had been disconnected. But he'd been known to let the phone bill get behind, so I didn't get really worried until my letters began to come back. Finally, I drove to the town where he had been living and found out that Tony had moved without leaving a return address. That's . . ." her voice cracked just a little, "that's when I realized what had happened."

"What did you do in the way of a search?"

"I filed a missing-person report with the police, of course. But as you probably know, it was hard to convince law enforcement agencies back then that people would really kidnap their own children.

"Once I even scraped together enough money to hire a private investigator. That's when I discovered that the first official record ever of Anthony Ward was a Michigan driver's license. The private detective told me that it was probably a fictitious name. I realized then that I had never even known my husband's real name. I *still* don't."

"Do you think you can help me, even without a real name?"

"It depends on whether the Social Security number he was using was valid."

"I tried *that* about twenty years ago," she said. "I sent a letter to Social Security, and the people there said they would forward the message and he could contact me if he wanted to. He never did, of course."

"Well, I have some resources that weren't available twenty years ago. I now have my pen in hand. Start giving me all the details you can remember."

As soon as I broke my connection with Elizabeth Kuhn, I punched the Social Security number she had given me into a database. What the Social Security Administration won't give out, even to the police in most instances, is available in private databases consisting of information sold to private research companies by credit bureaus and other companies. I got an immediate hit on the Social Security number. The accompanying date of birth was also a match. The name that came back with it was Paul Korda.

Obviously, Elizabeth's ex-husband had changed his name. But there's no law against changing your name, unless someone can prove that it was for the purpose of carrying out a fraudulent act. Some people change their names as often as their socks. Probable or not, however, it's a fair guess that a certain percentage of people who change their names do it to make themselves harder to find. It *is* harder. But it's not impossible.

Calling up another database, I soon had a current address and phone number for Paul Korda. The second database told me that he was connected with a real estate company in the Florida Keys. I decided to call him up and ask for his daughter Pamela's current address and phone number.

In my opinion, many of my colleagues waste a lot of time trying to pull off subterfuges. Entire books have been written on the subject. They will climb a tree to do something sneaky when they could just as easily—and more effectively—stand on the ground and tell the truth. It has usually been my experience that a direct question is the best way to get a usable answer. And you can always try something else if the straightforward approach doesn't work.

"Hello, Paul Korda speaking."

It was a very pleasant voice, the type of voice that puts a person at ease. "Mr. Korda, my name is Norma Tillman. I'm a private investigator, and I've been hired by your ex-wife, Elizabeth, to locate your daughter, Pamela."

"Well, it's about time," he said.

"You have no objections to putting them in touch?"

"Of course not. Pamela always wanted to know her mother, but Elizabeth told me that I was never to contact her after the divorce. She said Pamela resembled me so much that she couldn't bear to look at her anymore. I always thought it was terribly wrong of Elizabeth, but I never spoke badly of her to Pamela. I told her that her mother was a sick woman with severe emotional problems. I've always hoped that Elizabeth would mature emotionally one day so Pamela could have a relationship with her real mother."

Wait a minute, I thought. *Have I been had by a pathological liar trying to make her ex-husband look like a villain?* I thought there was a sure way to find out.

"Will you give me Pamela's current phone number, Mr. Korda?"

"Of course I will. You'll need her address too. Are you ready to copy this?"

Moments later, I had the information I needed—plus a healthy dose of suspicion. Things were going much too well. And at least one of the parents with whom I had spoken in the course of a half-hour was a consummate liar.

"Thank you very much, Mr. Korda."

"You're welcome. And if you ever decide to relocate in the Keys, you give me a call. I not only act as a broker here; I also own a large percentage of the real estate." He laughed pleasantly.

"I'll keep that in mind."

After we had ended the call, I took a deep breath and dialed the number Paul Korda had given me. The phone rang several times before a woman answered it. In the background I could hear a recording of jazz piano.

"Hello?"

"Is this Pamela Korda?"

"Yes," she said, a question in her voice.

"I've been hired by your mother, Elizabeth, to locate you. She would very much like to get in touch."

"What kind of sick joke is this?"

"It's no joke," I replied, startled by her reaction. It wasn't what I had expected.

"It just happens that my mother has been dead for forty years. Either there's been some kind of mistake, or you have to be pulling a horrible, tasteless joke."

"Pamela, I just spoke to your father, Paul Korda, about this matter. He's the one who gave me your telephone number."

"And he told you that my mother is alive?"

"I told him I had just spoken with her, and he said he thought it would be a great idea for you and your mother to get together."

Now her voice was definitely suspicious, and edged with hostility. "Give me your number—if you don't have anything to hide," she said. "I'm going to call my father right now and find out if you're lying!"

"I'd like you to do just that." I gave her my number and my address so she could verify the information through directory assistance if she wanted to. "But please get back to me and let me know what you find out. I assure you, I'm just as confused as you are."

I sat back and waited for the return call.

"Norma Tillman?"

"Yes," I replied, relieved to hear the voice at the other end. It had been less than an hour since I had spoken to Pamela Korda. The jazz was still playing on her end.

"I'm sorry for the way I talked to you a while ago," she said.

"Your father verified the story?"

"Yes."

"What had he told you before?"

"All my life he told me that my mother had died when I was

five. I remember when I was about ten, asking if I could visit my mother's grave."

"And what did he tell you?"

"He said there was no grave because she had been cremated."

"Well, what did he say this afternoon when you asked him about my phone call?"

"He said that one of my aunts—my mother's sister—had deceived him and that he had really believed my mother was dead all these years."

She paused for a moment. "Did he seemed surprised when you told him my mother was alive?"

"No. To the contrary. He told me that he had tried to get her to make contact with you ever since you were a little girl and that the only reason you hadn't met her was because she wasn't interested."

For several long seconds, all I could hear was the music.

"Norma," she finally asked, "do you think my mother's telling the truth?"

"So far, everything she has said has turned out be true."

"But why would my father lie to me like that? He didn't even act embarrassed. It's beyond reason!" Pamela said.

"I know, but your mother told me that your father always had a problem telling the truth. Korda isn't the name you were born with."

"I know. Ward is the name on my birth certificate. My father told me it was a typographical error that had never been corrected."

"It has to be hard on you to discover all these things in one afternoon."

She didn't seem to hear me. "For forty years I thought my mother was dead," she mused. "Then, out of the blue, I find out I could have talked to her anytime. It blows my mind."

"I can imagine," I said. Then, after a pause, I made the offer I often make to save my clients some money. "How would you like to meet your mother and have someone else pay all the expenses?" I asked.

"Who would do that?" she asked suspiciously.

"Any one of several national television shows," I told her. "I arrange reunions on shows like *Leeza*, *Oprah*, and a lot of others."

"I couldn't do that," Pamela said quickly. "I couldn't tell the story without letting the world know what a liar my father is. In fact, I still can't believe it myself. Why has he done this to me?"

"I don't know. I guess that telling lies is an addiction for some people. They can't seem to stop."

"Will you put me in touch with my mother? There are a lot of things I need to ask about."

"Of course I will. And if you change your mind about doing a television show, call me."

"Maybe," she said, the first sob causing her voice to crack. "Right now, having my mother back from the dead is about all I can handle."

And I had no trouble at all understanding exactly how she felt.

14

Like Dogs by the Side of the Road

THERE ARE THINGS that go on in this world that most people never hear about. And no doubt it's better that way. I can't see that society is improved by dwelling on the terrible things human beings do to one another.

But not everybody has the luxury of ignorance, the option of pretending that vile, unspeakable acts are mere echoes of insanity or infrequent occurrences in this family called humanity. Cops, medical personnel, and social workers—those whose professions put them in direct contact with suffering—have to cope with such knowledge on an almost daily basis.

I have seen the dark underbelly of human cruelty, first by working sexual abuse cases with a major metropolitan police unit, and later in my capacity as a private investigator.

The more my clients have suffered, the harder I am inclined to work on their cases when they seek my help. But sometimes, no matter how hard I try, there's little I can do to ease the pain or soften the raw injustice.

David came to me seeking help in finding his younger sister. The story he told me was one I'll never forget.

"My mother was a prostitute," David began that day, bitterness coloring his words as he was forced to dredge up things better forgotten. A man in his late thirties, thin and nervous, he twisted uneasily in his seat as he talked to me.

"There's no way to dress it up. She made a living by having sex with men. And it wasn't a case of a young girl taking up the profession just to get her through a hard time. She liked it. Or at least she liked it better than real work."

He paused and shrugged his shoulders.

"By the time I was old enough to have memories of my mother, the three oldest of her six children had already left. Maybe *escaped* is a better word. There were still three of us left at home then—me, my older brother, Doug, and our younger sister, Della. As you might imagine, our other brothers and sisters didn't come around very much.

"While other children were hunting Easter eggs and writing letters to Santa Claus, we were learning about sex. And I'm not talking about a lesson in the birds and the bees, complete with little books from the public library.

"All of us learned about sex by watching our mother work at home and by being actual participants when her perverted clients expressed an interest in having one or more of us join in. When we weren't having sex with a customer, we were all encouraged to have sex with each other for the entertainment of my mother and her friends and clients.

"We didn't know any better, of course. There was no shame involved when we were little. That came later—when we grew up and realized that normal people cherish their children and protect them from such things.

"Of course," David chuckled cynically, a sound that sent shivers up my spine, "messing us up sexually wasn't the worst thing she did—at least I don't think so.

"No, the worst thing she did happened after she had taken up with one man on a fairly regular basis. You'd think that would have improved our lives, wouldn't you? Instead of a parade of men, we just had to contend with Jeff.

"Of course, that was bad enough in itself. Jeff was a laborer who made good money when he worked." David's eyes seemed to grow cold as he remembered a long ago time. "He just didn't work very often. Every time it even looked like it might rain, or even if he just got a splinter in his finger, he stretched out on the couch and spent the rest of the day there, drinking beer and screaming at us.

"Jeff was always telling us how good things had been before he took up with a woman with a houseful of brats. He begrudged every penny that was spent feeding us or putting clothes on our backs.

"In spite of his abuse, though, I remember how terrified I used to become when Jeff would talk about making my mother choose between him or us. I had a pretty good idea what the outcome would be.

"And I was right. The whole thing finally came to a head one summer afternoon. Jeff told my mother point blank that she either had to get rid of us or find herself another man.

"Momma just kind of shrugged. Della was too young to understand what was going on, but Doug and I knew perfectly well. We hoped it would blow over—but it didn't.

"Later that day, Momma and Jeff walked into the room where all three of us shared a bed. 'Get your clothes on,' she told us. 'We're going to visit your brother Tom.'

"It was a relief, I remember, to hear her say that we were going to Tom's house. I had lived a long time with the fear that we would all be turned over to the authorities and end up in foster homes or an orphanage.

"Outside, Jeff ordered us all into the back of his old beat-up truck, where he hauled his beagles on hunting trips. Doug and I acted like we were just going for a drive in the country. We didn't want Della to know what was really going on.

"After what seemed like a long time, Jeff stopped the truck on a country road. Doug and I looked at each other in surprise as our mother got out of the cab. 'You kids jump out of the truck for a minute,' she said.

"Thinking that Jeff was having trouble with his old wreck of a truck, we lifted Della down, then stood and waited for him to go around and lift the hood. But he didn't. Our mother got back into the truck without saying a word.

"As they drove away, she never looked back. Not even once. Della began to cry, of course, and Doug and I did our best to comfort her, even though we were just scared little kids ourselves.

"After we walked for a little while, Doug paused at the end of a long driveway. Suddenly his eyes lit up. 'Look!' he yelled. 'It's Tom's house.'

"Sure enough, we had been dropped just down the road from our older brother's house. I figured out later that Momma already knew that Tom wouldn't let her leave us on his doorstep.

"Fortunately, we had walked in the right direction, instead of into the path of a car, or into the hands of somebody even worse than Momma and Jeff.

"Our happiness at finding Tom's house didn't last long. He didn't greet us with open arms, and his wife was even less friendly. Later, he took us aside and explained things to Doug and me, after Della was tucked in bed. He wouldn't look us in the eye.

"'Listen, I'd like t' help, but I got a baby with a heart condition. I just can't afford to take you guys in. Tomorrow I'm gonna have to call the people at Human Services and tell 'em that Momma has abandoned you.'

"My heart sank. What I was most afraid of had come to pass. The next day, we became official wards of the state. I don't know if the people at the state agency ever tried to find our mother, or if they just decided that a woman who left her children by the side of the road wouldn't be interested in taking them back."

David paused for a moment and looked me directly in the eye, as if trying to read my mind or possibly to gauge the kind of emotion his words had invoked in me.

"Fifteen years later, I went back and tracked down my mother and Jeff. I didn't really know *why* I wanted to see my mother again, but I knew I had to.

"I found them living in a rundown apartment house that smelled like beer and urine—pretty much like the kind of place we had lived in as children.

"When Jeff opened the door, it took him a second to realize who I was. He hadn't changed a.lot. His belly was bigger and he had less hair, but his mean expression hadn't changed at all.

"'What do *you* want?' he asked.

"As I stood there, it suddenly came to me why I had hunted them down. The rage boiled out.

"'What I want,' I said through clenched teeth, 'is to see the woman who gave birth to me, then left me standing like a dog by the side of the road. *That's* what I want!'

"Jeff stepped back, a little scared, I think, but with that sneer still in place. 'There's somebody here to see you,' he called back over his shoulder.

"'Who is it?'

"For the first time in fifteen years I heard my mother's voice. I think, maybe just for a moment, I expected some kind of feeling from her. Something that would show she was sorry.

"Jeff stepped aside and gave a sort of a bow, then he turned and left the room. My mother was lying on a ragged couch, wearing an old bathrobe. She looked at me with drunken, bleary eyes, lifted a can of beer to her lips, then set the can down on the floor before speaking.

"'What do *you* want?' she repeated. She might as well have been talking to a delivery boy.

"For maybe thirty seconds, I stood there with all the anger and hurt boiling inside. Then I turned and walked away without saying anything. There wasn't any point. My mother didn't mean anything at all to me anymore."

A silence fell over my office for a moment as David paused in his story. I heard the phone ring, then stop as my answering service picked up the call.

"That was thirty years ago," David finally continued. "I've since located Doug through the home where we lived after we were abandoned. But we can't find Della. Can you help us?"

Swallowing the lump in my throat, I nodded. "If she can be found, I'll find her."

I don't think I ever wanted to help anybody more than I wanted to help David—despite the fact that he had no money to pay me.

In a work of fiction, I would have found David's little sister. But this is a true story, and sometimes there the happy ending can't be staged. Eventually, I located a record of Della's marriage. Later, I found the man who had married and then divorced her. He sent me to the city where she had moved.

My final case notes tell the end of the story: "I found her apartment . . . empty . . . no forwarding address . . . no records . . . no trail." Reluctantly I had to mark the case closed.

A year later, long after I had marked David's file closed, I decided on a whim to call and follow up. I learned that in the year since the case was closed, David and Della had managed to find each other after all. Della's ex-husband had kept David's number, which I left with him, and had given it to Della when she happened to call.

In the end, it seems I was able to alleviate just a little bit of the pain that these siblings had endured. But ultimately there was nothing I could do, nothing anyone could do, to heal the wounds of three children whose mother had left them behind like dogs by the side of the road.

15

Deep, Dark Secrets

IT WAS A BEAUTIFUL house on the outskirts of Sacramento, a neighborhood inhabited by those with money and social connections. I had gone out to the house because the lady I was about to meet was concerned about her image. Apparently it just wouldn't do for such an important woman to be seen in the company of a common private detective.

She didn't put it that way, but I understood what she meant. And her attitude wasn't all that unusual. I knew from my days with law enforcement that battered women calling for help would sometimes demand that police cars arrive without sirens and lights. Even with their lives in danger, some people are still more worried about appearances than anything else.

The door was answered by a young Oriental woman wearing a traditional black-and-white housekeeper's uniform. I told her who I was, and she escorted me down a long hallway to a living room as large as some private dwellings. The original art on the walls, including what looked like a Van Gogh drawing, raised my estimate of the owner's personal fortune. My prospective client, a regal-looking woman in her mid-thirties with long legs and raven hair cascading down her back, stood and greeted me, a little nervously. That the matter involved her husband I had no doubt.

Less than two years earlier, there had been something of a scandal when a prominent banker had left his wife of twenty-five years to marry one of his tellers. I wondered whether history was about to repeat itself—or whether the dark-haired woman feared that such was the case.

"May I offer you something to drink?" she asked.

"No, thank you, Mrs. Plott. I have a busy schedule today. It would suit me if we could go directly to the heart of the matter."

"Very well," she said. "Please have a seat."

I settled in and waited. Sometimes you make progress by asking questions. At other times, you do so just by letting the client take the lead. Generally the problem will emerge with only a little prompting.

"Do you know who my husband is?"

"I'm as familiar with him as most people who keep up with the society page and the financial news, I guess."

"As you might imagine, the reputation of a financial adviser, especially one as prominent as my husband, is very important in maintaining the trust of his clients."

I nodded without comment. I had thought of him as a banker, but if "financial adviser" was the preferred title, it was all right with me.

"Well, of late my husband has been manifesting some serious symptoms of a, well, sexual nature."

"Yes?" My tone was businesslike. A private investigator has to show the same professional detachment as doctors, lawyers, psychiatrists, and others who come in contact with the hidden places of the human mind.

"Well, to be specific, he's been sleeping with prostitutes on a regular basis."

"I can see how that would concern you," I told her truthfully.

"Yes. Besides AIDS, there are a hundred other diseases he might carry home. I told him I wouldn't tolerate it. He moved out of our room several months ago—"

"I thought you said this had happened *of late*. How long a time period are we talking about?" I asked.

"Actually, it's been a lifelong problem, but I thought he had put it behind him when he married me. He just never seems to be satisfied sexually. And to be truthful, the things he had started asking for were getting more bizarre all the time."

"Have you tried talking to him about it?" I asked.

"Of course. He's been in therapy for a long time, but it doesn't seem to do any good."

"There are special clinics for sexual addictions, aren't there?"

"Yes, there are. But he has refused even to discuss going into any type of program that might put him in a hospital. He's afraid the press will get wind of it—and besides, he doesn't *really* think there's anything wrong with him."

"Is there any indication of how he developed this problem, or obsession, I guess, with prostitutes?"

"That's one of the few things we do know. When he was a teenager, he fell under the influence of an older woman, a neighbor who apparently made a hobby of seducing young boys. This woman was pretty kinky. The doctor says my husband is trying to re-live that first experience every time he goes to bed with a hooker."

"Well, since you've known this for some time, what has happened that was serious enough for you to seek my help? I'm sure it wasn't easy for you to involve a stranger in your life."

"Five days ago my husband left." There was a flash, barely noticeable, in her eyes as she made the statement.

"Where did he say he was going?"

"He *didn't*. He went to play golf with some of his colleagues. Halfway through the round, he excused himself and left. He hasn't contacted anyone since."

"And you want me to find him?"

"I know where he is. I want you to go there and persuade him to come home. If he thinks his secret is about to become public, I believe he'll come back."

"If you know where he is, why don't you just call him and tell him you're going to make it public?"

"I don't know *exactly* where he is, just the city he's in and the bar he's frequenting."

"How did you find that out?"

"He wrote a check for twenty-five thousand dollars to a top-less waitress in a Nevada dance hall because she told him she wanted to go back to school." A little color crept into Mrs. Plott's face, and the anger in her eyes had become pronounced. "She called his bank to see if the check was any good, and one of his associates called me."

"Was the check good?" I asked curiously.

"Of course it was good! And now that she's cashed it, the money is *hers*. He intends to spend every penny he's got because he thinks I'm going to divorce him."

The cat was out of the bag. Mrs. Plott, it seemed, was at least as concerned with the disposition of her husband's money as she was with his welfare.

"Just how much money are we talking about, Mrs. Plott?"

"He cashed in a quarter of a million dollars in stocks before he left," she said. "And I don't even know how much he drew out of his personal account. He keeps his personal money separate from what he gives me for household and living expenses."

In addition to the color in her face, a little bitterness had crept into her voice. I opened my purse and took out a pad and pen. "Why don't you give me all the details you have, and I'll see what I can do."

It looked as if I was about to become involved in an investigation that would be a little more interesting than most.

The Crystal Palace was not really a dance hall, as Mrs. Plott had described it. It was a semiprivate club featuring exotic dancers—one of a chain of many such across the western and southwestern United States that cater to wealthy and powerful men.

It was tucked behind a high chain-link fence and to enter I had to get by a uniformed security guard. The guard asked me whether I would be meeting someone, and when I said I would not, he seemed a little uneasy. I found out why when I talked to the manager a few minutes later.

The burly doorman with the slicked-back hair had called him the minute I arrived at the outer door. He was polite but firm when he told me that unescorted ladies were not encouraged at the Crystal Palace. Smiling politely in return, I produced my identification and introduced myself.

"How can I help you, Ms. Tillman?" the manager asked. He was well dressed and well groomed. He would not have seemed out of place as the manager of a fine hotel.

"I'm looking for this man." I produced a picture and showed it to him. He looked at it, then handed it to the doorman, who shook his head ruefully.

"We know him," the manager said. "He hasn't been here since the day before yesterday, but he'll more than likely show up again."

"Is it all right if I come in and talk to some of the dancers? I have reason to believe he may be with one of them."

"He was with one of my most popular dancers when he left here," the manager said. "He's pretty well disrupted business for the last few days."

"How?" I asked.

"Ms. Tillman, this is a high-roller club. The men who come in here think nothing of dropping a fifty- or a hundred-dollar tip to a dancer they like. But this guy has been handing over money by the handful, two and three hundred, sometimes even a thousand dollars at a time. The girls have been neglecting their other customers."

"I don't guess you'd tell me the name of the dancer he left with?" I asked.

"No. As management, I'm not supposed to give out information on any of our employees. But somebody else might tell you."

"Let me talk to your girls, then, and I may be able to get him out of your hair."

The manager thought it over for a minute, then nodded. "All right. I'm going to put you in an out-of-the-way place, because it puts a damper on business to have women here who aren't dancers or professional escorts. This is a fantasy world. My customers don't want to be reminded of the outside while they're here."

He quickly scanned the room, already in a hurry to return to other business. "Talk to the girls," he said, "but don't be obvious about it. And for heaven's sake, don't let any of my customers know you're a private eye! We run a discreet business here."

Nervously I followed the doorman to a table at the back of the darkened room, where multicolored lights softly blinked, apparently at random, producing a sort of other-worldly atmosphere. Even though I knew the nature of the club, the sheer size of it—there seemed to be half an acre of floor—and the fifteen to twenty healthy, seemingly unembarrassed, and almost completely naked young women gyrating to the music overwhelmed me just a little.

My original impulse was to look *away* from the girls. It was an attitude I got over quickly, once I got to know some of the dancers and realized they took pride in their performances. A few had even been classical dancers before taking up their present line of work.

"Can I get you something?" The waitress's costume was scanty, but I was relieved she at least had something on. She tried to hide her curiosity about why I was there, but not very successfully.

"I'd like a Coke, and I'd appreciate it if you'd take a look at this picture and tell me if you have ever seen this man." I laid the photograph out on the table.

"You a cop?" she asked.

"No, I'm a private investigator. Your manager knows why I'm here." The last sentence seemed to put her more at ease.

"Sure, I know him. He tipped me a hundred bucks one night. And he's been dropping a thousand dollars at a time to the dancers for private dances."

Seeing that I seemed puzzled, she smiled and pointed to a table not far away. There, a beautiful young woman was dancing on what looked like a small stool, right beside the table. She was moving her body perhaps six inches from the customer's face. He seemed oblivious to everything but the girl. It was then that I noticed for the first time that only a few girls were up on the performance stages at any given time, while most were at the various tables.

"Everybody takes turns on stage," the waitress said. "But the money is made in the private dances at the tables. The dancers don't draw a salary, you know. Their entire income is tips. For the length of a couple of songs, the customer has a private performance. The girls can get close, but touching is against the rules."

"Do the girls . . . do they ever . . . ?"

"They're not supposed to." The waitress laughed. "If there's enough money involved, though, some will go out with a customer after hours."

"Thank you," I told her. "Would you pass the word why I'm here and tell the dancers I'd like to talk to them?"

"Why do you want to find this man?"

"I'm not at liberty to say. You wouldn't have any information, would you?"

"He's out with a dancer by the name of Terry Frost. She left with him the day before yesterday, and she hasn't been to work since."

"No secret about it, then?"

"None at all. A lot of the other dancers are jealous because he picked her. And we've all been curious about what's going on. Terry hasn't answered her phone. And missing work without calling in . . . well, the management sort of frowns on that, if you know what I mean."

"Well, I'd still like to speak with anyone who will talk to me. You never know what someone might have noticed."

The time I spent in the club was a real learning experience, the kind of adventure that makes me glad I do what I do instead of selling cosmetics or working in a store. There's nothing wrong with either of those jobs, but there's little likelihood that an Avon lady or a store clerk will ever get to fly to Nevada and hang out in a strip joint.

At first the dancers seemed wary of me. After a few hours, though, they began to stop by my table, mostly out of curiosity, I think. The Crystal Palace, I learned, was part of a large circuit followed by three hundred of the most beautiful strippers in the country. The standard for such dancers was high. The women had to have poise and an air of class as well as good looks. Most were wholesome looking, all-American, girl-next-door types. Tattoos and extreme hairstyles, it was explained, were not allowed.

It was a surprise to me that young women who routinely stripped down to a tiny G-string for their customers seemed so well balanced and, in some cases, well educated. I might also add that they were well paid.

"I just bought a home that's worth over a hundred thousand dollars," one buxom redhead told me. "My son goes to a private school. What other work could I find that would pay like this? I'm not ashamed of what I do. The customers can *look*, but that's all they can do. My life away from here is totally separate from what I do for a living."

Of course, not all the women felt the same way. Several of them verified what the waitress had told me. If the customer looked good and the money was right, many of them supplemented their incomes by practicing the world's oldest profession part time.

The customers were almost as much of a surprise as the dancers themselves. I had always assumed that the type of men who frequented strip joints would be loud, redneck, and lower class. But such was not the case at the Crystal Palace.

The customers were well dressed and well behaved. Most looked like successful businessmen. The majority were in their forties and fifties, though younger men tended to show up later in the evenings, probably after work.

In all, I spent the better part of two days watching the activities and soaking up the atmosphere. I began to feel almost like a mother or a big sister to some of the women during that time. But Mr. Plott, the mysterious, big-spending banker, never did show up.

When I got back to my motel after the second day in Nevada, I found out why. There was a message for me to call Mrs. Plott. I learned that the banker had called his brother from a hotel room in New Orleans (one that he was sharing with the wayward stripper named Terry, who had just made a sizable deposit in her bank account). The brother had flown down and persuaded the banker to check into a sexual addiction clinic before all his money was squandered—though as it turned out, it was too late for that.

Mrs. Plott told me that my services were no longer needed, and I should send her a final bill. I did so, and my check arrived promptly by messenger. As far as I knew at that moment, my connection with the freewheeling banker was finished. In my business, however, nothing is certain.

≈ ≈ ≈

"Excuse me," said the voice. "Aren't you Norma Tillman, the private investigator?"

I turned in the airport waiting area and found the speaker to be a handsome man, perhaps in his early fifties, expensively dressed. I knew at once that I should recognize him, but his identity eluded me for a few moments.

"I'm Brad Plott," he said with the eager air of someone greeting a new business acquaintance at a convention. "My wife hired you to track me down a couple of years ago, in Nevada."

"Yes, I remember," I said somewhat hesitantly, knowing that *he* knew that *I* knew deep, dark secrets about him. He apparently picked up on my nervousness and immediately moved to put me at ease.

"Don't be embarrassed." He smiled, showing even white teeth. "I was a sick man. Now I'm recovered. Such things happen."

"How did you recognize *me?*" I stammered.

"I've seen you on a couple of television shows. Are you here in Los Angeles to tape another one?"

"No, actually I was here to discuss a possible movie deal."

"The movie won't be about me, will it?" He laughed as if we were old friends.

"No, but yours was a very interesting case, I must admit. How is Mrs. Plott, by the way?"

"The last I heard she was back in the hick town where she was born, working as a waitress. When my finances hit bottom and we lost the house and she saw there was nothing left for her to squeeze out of me, she filed for divorce."

I only nodded, offering no comment.

"Well, it was nice to finally meet you, but I have a plane to catch."

We shook hands and I watched him get in line at the loading gate. In the ten minutes or so that followed, I saw him strike up a conversation with an attractive woman young enough to be his daughter. When they went through the gate, his hand was on her arm and she was already staring up at him with stars in her eyes. Regardless of his deep, dark secrets, he *was* a charming man.

16

Fanning Old Flames

VOLUMES HAVE BEEN WRITTEN about the concept of long-lost loves, of passions that smolder for years and years and then burst into flames when the lovers are reunited. The theme has been a favorite of poets and screenwriters alike. Contemporary newspapers, too, love to run stories of lost loves reunited after many years. In reality, though, old flames are sometimes quite different from the warm, rose-colored memories we carry around.

Several years ago, Charles Bronson and Jill Ireland costarred in a movie called *From Noon till Three*. It was about a small-time outlaw who broke into a house while on the run from the law. The resident of the house (Ireland's character) was at first aghast at the idea of having an outlaw in her house. But then she quickly fell into Bronson's arms for a short, passionate affair—three hours, to be exact.

When Bronson's character left the house to meet his partners in crime, he was captured and sent to the penitentiary—under an alias, as I recall.

Ireland's character, after realizing that her one true love was not going to return, wrote a book about their afternoon of delight. The book rapidly became a national bestseller, turning her and Bronson's character into household names on a par with Romeo and Juliet.

From prison, Bronson's somewhat cynical character read the highly romanticized book, listened to discussions by his cellmates, and observed the growing phenomenon with a jaundiced eye.

By the time he got out of prison, every theater and touring company in America was doing a play based on the book. A song about the love affair was on everyone's lips. And the house where the story took place had been turned into a shrine, with regular tours given by Ireland's character.

Bronson's character, upon release from prison, immediately proceeded to the house. In disguise, he joined one of the guided tours. Waiting until the tour group was gone, Bronson took off his fake beard and stood before Ireland's character, smiling.

He waited to be recognized, and when he wasn't, he finally told her who he was. Ireland's character haughtily informed him that the love of her life had been over six feet tall and the hand-somest man she had ever met—characteristics not shared by Bronson.

Eventually, by giving her details that only the two of them could have known, he convinced her that he was indeed the man with whom she had shared a passionate interlude. Faced with the truth as opposed to her romantic memory, Ireland's character couldn't go on. She chose to die rather than accept things as they were—or as they had really been.

Bronson's character, finally driven berserk by the song and the constant reminders of the book, was, in the last scene, taken to an insane asylum and introduced to those who also thought they were famous historical characters, like Caesar and Napoleon. The concept was perhaps a little exaggerated for artistic purposes, but maybe not as much as most romantics would like to believe.

A male colleague of mine tells a story about a young woman with whom he became infatuated in high school. He never got up enough nerve to ask her out. From afar, however, he admired the cool, calm way she responded to questions and the regal way she walked from one class to another, obviously thinking on deep subjects, with a look of serenity on her face.

Thirty years later, he happened upon this same woman in a supermarket. She was still stunningly beautiful. My friend, having risen to a high level of success in his own field, was finally able to muster the confidence to strike up a conversation with her. It only took a couple of minutes for his fantasy of the cool, aloof, and serenely thoughtful woman to dissolve.

"What I had once taken for a calm, sophisticated mode of behavior was actually an inability to comprehend simple sentences," my friend told me later. "Her regal manner was not due to deep thought but to a total lack of it.

"Not only did she not remember me, she had trouble remembering what year we graduated from high school and the young man with whom she went steady for two years. If I had asked, she probably wouldn't have remembered the Vietnam War.

"I talked with her for a few minutes, trying to reminisce about things we had in common. I guess I was desperately trying to salvage just a little of my fantasy. But it didn't work.

"When we parted company, I regretted that I had run into her. The image I had carried around for thirty years was preferable to the reality of what I learned about her."

My friend, bright as he is, had been a victim—maybe a willing victim—of selective amnesia. On some level he probably knew, even in high school, that the girl was all fluff and no substance, but he chose to overlook and forget those aspects of her that didn't fit his fantasy. And there was nothing necessarily wrong with that. We all need our fantasy memories to keep us warm sometimes.

That's why I jumped at the chance to take part in a *Vicki Lawrence Show* dedicated to reuniting people with their first loves—or at least the people they *remembered* as their first loves. My good friend Bonnie Tiegel produced the show. It wasn't the first or the last show done on that theme, but I had a great time doing it. To me, it was a revealing experiment in fantasy, memory, and human nature.

Of the four couples who appeared on the show, three participated as a result of searches launched at the requests of the women. But the gender of the searcher didn't really make a difference; the results were the same. Almost invariably, those who wanted to find a lost love all had more vivid memories of the love affairs than did the person who was sought.

Brad and Melissa hadn't seen each other in twenty-seven years. Brad remembered romantic trips to drive-in movie theaters and a trip to a Beatles concert. His story was full of romantic details, including the fact that he had given Melissa his precious collection of celebrity autographs.

It was obvious that Brad really thought of Melissa as "the one"—the woman he should have married. To his recollection, Melissa had taken up with someone else while he was going through basic training in the Air Force.

Melissa, an attractive woman in her mid-forties, was obviously uncomfortable with the whole "lost love" scenario. Happily married, she had arrived with her husband's blessing. And it was obvious that she only vaguely recalled most of the incidents that had remained so vivid for Brad. Her recollection of her time with Brad seemed to be that the two of them were friends and that even though she was otherwise involved, she had taken the time to spend a day with him when he was home on leave from basic training. The precious autograph collection had been burned in a house fire—the only old flame that Melissa intended to discuss that day.

Carolyn, in her middle to late fifties, had been carrying a torch for Richard more than forty years. "I don't take rejection well," she told Vicki.

Carolyn's warm memories went back to a time when she was a fifteen-year-old girl in love with Richard, a minor-league ball player who was only eighteen himself. She recalled long, romantic walks from the ballfield to her house for dinner and lingering conversations on the front steps. Carolyn had even saved a souvenir—an autographed baseball from a winning game—that Richard had given her. It was easy to see that for her the old flame of romance was still burning cheerily.

Carolyn recounted that Richard, returning to town five years later, had called looking for her, but that her mother had not passed the message along because Carolyn was at the hospital having her first baby. Even now, many years later, she regarded that missed call as a missed opportunity.

Richard, on the other hand, only *vaguely* remembered Carolyn. He indicated that at the time he was a young man with very little money and that he pretty much took his meals where he could get them.

He acknowledged that he had signed the baseball and that he should have remembered a winning game because he hadn't experienced too many of them! And I don't think he even remembered making a phone call five years later. If he did, he wasn't overly concerned about it.

Susan had been carrying a torch for Bob since her college days in Daytona Beach, Florida, when the two of them had walked together on the boardwalk. She had carefully preserved photographs and written mementos of the handsome young lifeguard. Among the memorabilia were a locket he had given her and a letter he had written, which said that even though he had had many relationships, she was the one he still thought about.

Bob obviously remembered Susan fondly, but you couldn't watch without realizing that his memories of her had not been smoldering, waiting for an opportunity to spring back to life as hers had. It was pretty obvious that he didn't remember writing the last letter. And whether or not he actually remembered the locket seemed doubtful.

Susan hid her disappointment well; after all, she was on national TV. But as I watched her I thought I saw a sad little flicker of a fantasy dying.

≈ ≈ ≈

Amy and Ted had been high-school sweethearts, and they hadn't seen each other in almost thirty-five years. You could see the fond memories in Amy's eyes as Ted uncomfortably walked out on the stage.

A stocky, down-to-earth type, Ted seemed a little bewildered. There was no doubt that he remembered Amy. But he obviously had not spent a lifetime recalling the night of their prom, as she had.

Ted did well under the circumstances, I think, but his memory was simply blank about many things Amy remembered vividly. She had told me that she and Ted had even worn the same kind of sweaters when they were high-school students. Ted confirmed that they had indeed dressed alike. But when Amy challenged him to tell her the color of their sweaters, he just couldn't recall. Neither did he remember the perfume he had given her on prom night or the little program book in which she had recorded her dances—all of them with Ted.

Both of them, however, seemed relatively pleased with the encounter. Neither was married, and Ted acknowledged that he was "available" after two years as a widower.

Who knows? Maybe this was one long-carried torch that might eventually burst back into flames. I hope so. I've seen a lot of romantic disappointment over the years, but I've also seen a lot of happy endings. Besides, like most people, I'm a sucker for a good love story.

17

A Brother's Oriental Bride

Dear Norma,

   *My husband, Ken, would love to find his older brother,
Bill, who disappeared over twenty years ago after a family
dispute. Ken was twelve the last time he saw his brother.
Bill married a Korean woman while he was in the Army,
and his mother told him that his bride was not welcome.
He never returned home or contacted anyone again. The
only information I have is his name and Social Security
number. . . .*

Lonely soldiers fall in love with local girls. It's a fact borne out
by history. Marriage between Roman legionnaires and native
women was so prevalent in ancient times that special cities grew
up around the practice. These cities were called *coloniae* to signify
that the inhabitants were true citizens of Rome.

Romance and human nature have not changed since the days
of the Roman legions. Wherever young men are stationed, they
still tend to fall in love with local girls. Often they marry them
and bring them home. And though many such marriages turn out
to be happy, the couples do face special challenges in addition to
the normal adjustments of marriage. A woman who marries a soldier from another country has to contend with new customs and
sometimes a new language. And she faces the prospect of being

an outsider in her new family, which might not welcome her with open arms. Such, I would learn during my investigation, was the case with my client's brother-in-law, that young soldier by the name of Bill.

Hoping that his family would share with him the most important event in his life, he had gone home to the small rural community where he grew up and told his mother about her new daughter-in-law, a young Korean woman who would soon be following him to America. But instead of the joyous smile and open arms he had hoped for, Bill encountered his mother's fury. Screaming and irrational, she informed him that his foreign wife would *never* be welcome at her home and that he was never to bring the young woman there. He took her at her word, and no one in the family had ever heard from Bill again.

My client, Linda, was concerned because she had *only* Bill's name and his Social Security number. She had no way of knowing, of course, that a true name and a Social Security number are two of the most valuable pieces of information one can have when searching for a lost friend or loved one.

The fact is, most "lost" people are not really lost; they simply don't know that other people are looking for them. Such people have no reason to try to cover the trail of documents that we all leave every time we make a purchase, place a telephone call, or apply for a license, to name but a few signposts on the paper trail.

If a person is hiding intentionally, that throws an entirely different light on the matter. Those with criminal intent will usually operate under a fictitious name and sometimes a fraudulent Social Security number. And such people can be quite difficult, though not impossible, to locate.

With the real name and the correct Social Security number, I located Bill in just a few minutes spent cruising the great information superhighway. Bill was in a West Coast city.

I hit my first speed bump on the highway when I couldn't find
a telephone number for Bill. It was only a minor slowdown, however, because his neighbors had telephones. It only took a short
side trip into another database to acquire a few of those numbers.
A couple of calls later, I had the name of the manager of his
apartment complex.

"Pacific Rentals. Sharon Wilson speaking."

"Ms. Wilson, my name is Norma Tillman. I'm a private investigator based in Nashville, Tennessee. My client is a sister-in-law
of one of your tenants, a Bill Blackman. Her husband and his
brother haven't seen each other in twenty years. Can you help
me get in touch with Mr. Blackman?"

"Who are you again?"

"My name is Norma Tillman. I've been hired by Mr. Blackman's sister-in-law to locate him."

"I'm not allowed to give out private information, Ms. Tillman.
But if you'll leave a telephone number, I'll see that Mr. Blackman
gets the message."

"Thank you very much. My number is. . . ."

I hadn't really expected her to give me the number. Having
her relay a message was the best I had hoped for. But it never
hurts to ask. Sometimes people will rattle off everything you
need with very little prompting. In any case, I was pretty sure the
apartment manager would pass along the number. I had heard
the note of intrigue in her voice. I sincerely hoped Bill would get
back to me quickly, because I had a special plan for him and
Ken. But time was of the essence.

"Norma Tillman speaking."

"Ms. Tillman?" The man at the other end of the phone sounded hesitant. "My apartment manager left a message that you are
trying to contact me. I'm Bill Blackman."

"Mr. Blackman, thanks so much for getting back so quickly.

Your younger brother, Ken, would like to talk to you."

"Uh, Ms. Tillman, no offense intended, but I find it hard to believe that *anyone* in my family would be looking for me after all these years—not after the way I've treated them."

"Ken most definitely wants to contact you. He's still living in Trenton. His wife, Linda, is the person who actually wrote me on his behalf. He told her you had married a Korean woman and that your mother had ordered you out of the house and told you never to come back. Linda says Bill was about twelve then and that he's worried about you ever since."

There was silence at the other end of the line, then I heard faintly the chest-wrenching sobs of a man trying very hard to control himself. I waited until he was ready to talk again.

"I'm sorry," he said. "Your call was such a shock. I had always thought the rest of my family would probably be angry with me because I broke off contact with them. It never occurred to me that they might want to talk to me again."

"Oh, rest assured that they do." Then I sprung my surprise. "Mr. Blackman, how would you like to actually see Ken in person?"

"That would be great, but, well, I can't afford to travel."

"What if I could arrange an all-expenses-paid trip?"

The line was silent for several seconds. "What's the catch?" he then asked, a tremor of hope in his voice.

"A very small catch," I told him laughingly. "I've been talking to the producer of a nationally syndicated daytime talk show. She is planning a reunion special, a show where lost loved ones can be reunited on the air. If you would be willing to meet your brother on the show, they will pay all your expenses."

"Has Ken agreed?" Bill asked.

"No. I wanted to get your reaction first. If you had asked me not to give Ken your address, I would have abided by your wishes. My job is to help people, not cause them problems."

Another short silence. "Well, if Ken is willing, then so am I."

"Great!" I said. "I'll be back in touch as soon as I can make the arrangements."

"I'm sorry," the hollow-sounding recording said, "but the number you have reached has been changed to an unlisted number."

For a moment I sat stunned. I carefully looked at the number that Ken's wife had sent me so recently. I dialed it again—just to be sure—and got the same recording.

Later, I would discover that it had been a simple mix-up. Linda had asked for a new number but was not expecting the change for several days.

Things began to look dim for the proposed reunion. After a few minutes of self-pity, I shook myself out of the doldrums. *Norma*, I said to myself, *you're a detective who locates people every day. Get busy and find out how to contact Linda.*

An hour later, I was very frustrated. The address Linda had given me was correct, but my normal methods of locating neighbors was not working. Not only was the address in a rural area, but it was also on a state highway without regular street numbers. If I started calling people, I would eventually find someone who knew Ken or his wife. But it would be long and tedious task, and I didn't have a lot of time.

Then, without warning, inspiration struck. I called the operator and asked for the local sheriff's department in Ken's hometown.

"This is Norma Tillman," I told the sergeant at the other end of the line. "I know this sounds strange, but I'm a private investigator from Nashville, Tennessee. I'm trying to locate a Ken Blackman so I can deliver a message to him. He lives on Highway 61, somewhere in your county. The only other thing I know about him is that he has a wife by the name of Linda. I know that's not much to go on, but. . . ."

"Could you hold on just a minute, ma'am?" There was click at the other end as I was put on hold.

"Certainly," I said into the silent phone, then waited.

After ten minutes, I was ready to hang up. It had been too much to ask, even of a sheriff's department in a small town. I had been silly to make the call. The sergeant was probably having a good laugh at my expense. I had just decided to break the connection when the sergeant came back on the line.

"Ms. Tillman?"

"Yes?"

"I sent a car up to Ken Blackman's house. The officer's talkin' to Ken right now. What was the message you wanted to give him?"

At such moments I really do believe in miracles.

It was a joyful reunion. The siblings, who had not seen each other for more than twenty years, wept and hugged each other without shame. Linda Blackman, who had never met her brother-in-law, wept too. As for me, I had a big smile on my face. Such reunions are what I strive for, the reason I stay in this business, and the reason I enjoy what I do. I can't end this story, however, without telling you something else that happened the day before the show.

While Ken and his brother had talked on the phone prior to the trip, they had agreed not to see each other until the television reunion. Upon arriving in the city where the filming would take place—a city where neither had ever been before—each of them procured a map of local attractions. Both decided to visit the same museum that afternoon. So, for at least two hours, Bill and Ken walked around that museum at the same time, looking at the same exhibits—passing each other several times. Of course, they didn't realize it until they came face to face the next day.

What are the odds of two long-separated brothers choosing the same destination on the same evening in a city of millions that neither had ever visited before? I don't know about you, but such an incident boggles my imagination. And I'm used to surprises.

18

Sometimes the Answer Is Out of Reach

JUST AFTER MIDNIGHT, Maria drove her vehicle onto the shoulder of the rural Texas road. It seemed unlikely that anyone would disturb her in such an isolated area. She had taken great pains to get away from possible interruptions.

The young mother got out of her vehicle and looked at her two little girls, one five and the other seven. They were both dozing fitfully in the back seat. Neither awoke as she made preparations to carry out the horrible task she had set for herself.

Everything that she could do to protect her children had been done. Now she was out of resources. Despite her appeal to the court to keep her children from their father, he had been given unsupervised visitation rights.

Their father, a powerful corporate executive who had already raised one set of children before marrying Maria and beginning a second family, seemingly could not be stopped. Maria was certain he had been sexually abusing the older girl. Even if the younger had been spared thus far, it was only a matter of time until she also fell victim.

Nobody had believed Maria. That such a successful and respected businessman, a pillar of the community, could be guilty of unthinkable behavior was beyond belief to most people.

The young mother, blinded by grief and worry, had decided that a quick, painless death was better than the agony of turning her children over to a man who would rob them of their innocence for his perverted pleasure.

She had cried so much in recent months. Now she seemed to be beyond tears. Clear-eyed, she opened the trunk and removed the hose and duct tape she had bought earlier at a hardware store. It took only a few minutes for her to secure the hose to the exhaust pipe and run it through the front window. Inside the car, she carefully sealed the window around the hose with the duct tape.

Maria started the engine and waited, certain that she and her two children would awaken in a better place. *Just a little while longer and the nightmare will be over*, she told herself as she drifted into unconsciousness.

She awoke in a hospital emergency room, bright lights blinding her, sympathetic voices explaining what had happened. She and her children had been lucky, she was told. Another driver, lost and looking for a remote address, had happened to pass her vehicle. Quickly assessing the situation, he had opened the doors, turned off the engine, and gone for help. All three of them had survived the carbon monoxide poisoning.

And Maria didn't need to worry about the children, the nurses told her cheerily. Her husband had come to pick them up. The distraught young mother could see them again when she was well—after she got out of the psychiatric ward.

The real nightmare was just beginning.

"Norma Tillman," I said into the receiver, still focusing on the screen of my computer. "How may I help you?"

"Norma, this is Charles Baldwin. I need a little assistance from you on a case I'm working."

"Let me guess. It has to do with a missing person or persons. Right?"

"That's your specialty, isn't it?" He laughed. Charlie and I go back a long way. He is an ethical man and a good investigator.

"Charlie, this wouldn't be another one of those clients who can't pay, would it?"

"Well, Norma, let's just say that she can't pay the kind of money I usually charge. But it's a worthy cause."

"All right, let's hear it." Worthy causes can kill you financially. But there are times when the moral issue outweighs the monetary factor.

"Five years ago my client got a divorce. Her ex-husband was a very powerful man. She suspected that he was molesting one of their daughters, maybe both of them, but she couldn't get anyone to listen to her. She says—and you can take it for what it's worth—that he was able to hinder the actual police investigation."

"That wouldn't be unheard of, would it?" I asked. Most cops are decent, upright people, but every profession has its bad apples.

"My client had a nervous breakdown—I guess that's what you'd call it. She tried to gas herself and the two girls with carbon monoxide."

"That brings up another question, then. Is your client fit to have custody?"

"I think so. We have letters from two psychiatrists stating that she's sane and that her previous behavior is not likely to recur. Her husband got temporary custody while she was in treatment. Then, after she got out and began to file motions for the return of her children, he took the kids and vanished. There are warrants on him for kidnapping."

"How are they living?" I asked, feeling myself being slowly drawn in.

"He's retired from a major corporation. His pension is more than four thousand dollars a month," Charlie said.

"The check is mailed to him somewhere, right?"

"Already checked that. All his mail goes to a box rented by his sister in North Dakota. She's apparently running it though her own accounts and forwarding it to him. I have reason to believe that he and the girls are living on the move in a camper."

"Charlie, I've got a lot of cases of my own."

"You're the *only* person I know with the kind of background it's going to take to find these girls."

"All right, Charlie. Send me the file, and I'll take a look at it."

A few days later I sat in my office and looked through the file that Charlie Baldwin had forwarded to me. I could see that he had done a thorough job.

There were pictures of the two girls as they had looked just before they were snatched, all gleaming dark hair and big brown eyes. If the mother was right about what had happened to them— I shuddered, not wanting to think what they might have been subjected to during the next few years.

Also enclosed were the computer printouts for the arrest warrant from the National Crime Information Center and from the database where Charlie had unsuccessfully checked for Social Security number activity. There had been no activity on the suspect's Social Security number or the numbers of his two children. That meant one of two things. Either he was making only cash transactions, or he had somehow acquired another Social Security number. The first was more likely.

Neither had the suspect presented his driver's license anywhere during the period he had been missing. Charlie had found that out by having someone in a law enforcement agency conduct what is known as an "off-line search." Any inquiry made about an individual through the national law enforcement database comes up on such a search.

There were two items in the file that I knew would require closer investigation. I needed more details on the suspected kidnapper's sister, and I intended to travel to Los Angeles and look at the file compiled by a national television show on which the two girls had been featured as missing. It was going to be, I feared, a long and expensive search. I agreed with Charlie that it was a worthy cause. I just hoped it wasn't a lost cause.

≈ ≈ ≈

Parked alongside the dusty road in western New Mexico, I watched the two young girls as they hoed between rows of corn on the communal property of a group called the New Ark of the Covenant. They seemed about the right ages, ten and twelve, and their coloring was right. But children can change so much in five years.

After three weeks of being involved in the search for Maria's daughters, I had found myself staring at every little dark-haired girl I met, wondering how the two children in the picture were faring. I had come to New Mexico as the result of what I had found in the file reluctantly shown to me by the producers of the television show.

Apparently, the people who put on the show had only been interested in "gimmes," or those cases where people would call up and tell them for sure where to find a lost child. Certainly they had not put any time into a serious investigation of the leads that had been called in from around the country.

In the file, I had found notes indicating that four people had called with possible information on the missing children. Two claimed to have seen the father and daughters at campgrounds— one in Colorado and one in Nevada. Two others indicated that they might have seen the girls and their father at religious gatherings put on by a fringe group of which I had heard but was not familiar—the New Covenant of the Ark.

A little browsing at the library had produced information that the New Covenant of the Ark group had several hundred members nationwide and that their "mother church" was just outside a sleepy little New Mexico town. Their doctrine was a mishmash of Old and New Testament teachings. Like so many other religious fringe groups, the members were preparing for Armageddon.

I had flown in two days earlier and taken a room in the small town near the commune. A trip to the courthouse had led me to the building permits and blueprints filed by the commune's members when they built their Ark of the Covenant, or rather the

building in which it was housed. There was also an artist's render-
ing of the commune's streets and individual housing units.

A visit with the local chief of police to touch base and show
him pictures of the girls and their father produced little new
information.

"Basically," the chief told me, "the cult members keep to
themselves. Only a few of them come out to do the shopping and
whatever else needs to be done. The children and their father
could have been there, or they could be there now and I wouldn't
know it."

It was pretty obvious to me that the chief, an elderly man
retired from a larger police department, had had no problems
with the cult and wanted to keep it that way. He hadn't said that
in so many words, but there was satisfaction in his voice when he
noted that the cult members *keep to themselves*.

After my research was done, I had decided to drive out to the
commune and present myself in person. That was how I had
come to be parked outside the cult headquarters. I took one last
look at the two young girls hoeing in the cornfield, drew a deep
breath, started my car, and drove around to the front gate.

The commune area consisted of neatly painted white cinder-
block houses. Each had a small garden beside it, in addition to the
fields of corn surrounding the housing units. I stopped my car in
front of the Ark of the Covenant building, which was different
from the others only in that it was bigger than most, and got out.

"Excuse me," I said to a girl of sixteen or so who had just
walked around from the rear of the large building. She was wearing a homemade cotton dress, and her yellow hair was drawn
back in pigtails. She carried a basket of tomatoes under her right
arm. She paused, then looked around, as if not quite sure whether
she should speak to me. Finally she walked over.

"My name is Norma Tillman." I showed her my identification.
"I wonder if you could look at some pictures for me." I handed her
the photo of the two small girls and one of their father. She stared
at the pictures for a moment. Her eyebrows went up as if in sur-

prise, but before she could speak a voice boomed from the front door of the building.

"Is there something I can do for you? I am the Keeper of the Ark." I had expected someone in robes and a long white beard. However, this man was perhaps fifty, with neatly trimmed gray hair. "Libby, you can go along. I'll talk to the lady," he said.

The girl handed back the pictures, eyes lowered, refusing to return my gaze, as the man walked in my direction.

"How may I help you?" he asked. Up close, I was struck by his startling blue eyes and his air of authority. It was easy to imagine him mesmerizing a congregation.

"I'm looking for these two children and their father." I handed him the photographs. "The man in the picture is accused of kidnapping his daughters."

"What does that have to do with us?" The man stared directly into my eyes, revealing nothing.

"I have information indicating that he may have attended services put on by your church."

"Many come to us seeking truth," he told me. "We do not ask for credentials."

"All right, let me put it another way. Has this man been here, or is he here now with the children?"

"No." I thought I detected a flash of anger way back in his eyes, but it was hard to tell. "Now, if you will excuse me—"

"Would you mind if I talked to some of your members?" I asked.

"Yes, I *would* mind. The world does not intrude here any more often than I can prevent it."

"If you have nothing to hide—"

"I have nothing to hide! Do you have a warrant?"

"No," I replied.

"Then please leave." He turned and walked stiffly through the door.

I sighed and got back into my rental car. As I turned left through the gate, I saw someone waving from beside the road, under the low-hanging branches of a small clump of trees. It was the girl with the pigtails. I wondered how she had gotten outside the fence without passing me. I slowed down as she ran up to the vehicle.

"They're here!" She said in a whisper. "No, don't stop. If they see me, I'm in trouble. The man and the little girls live here. Get the little girls away if you can!"

Before I could reply, she turned and darted back into the thicket of trees. What had compelled her, I wondered, to betray the members of her cult?

Having already met the local law, I decided that it would be pointless to ask for assistance. If my judgment of the chief had been accurate, the best I could hope for was for him to refuse assistance. At worst, I feared he would tip off the cult leader. I drove to the nearest city with an FBI field office and asked to speak to someone about a matter of importance. A few minutes later, wearing a badge marked visitor, I was introduced to a young man who took notes and nodded attentively as I told my story.

"Ms. Tillman, we appreciate that you've taken the time to bring this information to us. We'll handle things from here."

"Will you get in touch with Mr. Baldwin when you have the children in custody?" I asked. "It *is* his case."

"I can assure you that we'll do whatever is required," he told me with a smile.

For the first time since Charlie had sent me the file, I slept well that night, certain that the ordeal would soon be over for the little girls. I should have called Charlie to inform him of what had transpired, but everything seemed to be going all right, and I was behind in my work. So the next day I returned home and moved on to catch up the backlog of cases that had piled up while I was looking for the two children. I gave the case no further thought until Charlie called a week later.

"Norma, this is Charlie Baldwin," he said without preliminaries, as soon as I answered the telephone.

As soon as I heard the tone of Charlie's voice, I knew something was not right. I hoped the man had not moved on with the girls before the FBI had acted—especially in light of the fact that I might have caused him to bolt by asking questions at the commune.

"For a detective with a solved case, you don't sound very happy. Does your client have her children back yet?" I asked hopefully.

"That's what I'm calling about."

"Hasn't the FBI been in touch with you?"

"No, but it's strange that you should ask. I was updating my file, so I contacted the DA's office. Seems that the kidnapping warrant for Maria's ex-husband isn't on the national crime computer. It's been deleted."

"What happened?" I asked him. "I found them at a religious commune in New Mexico and turned the case over to the closest FBI field office."

Charlie's silence at the other end was eloquent. Suddenly the import of what he had said began to sink in.

"I guess this case really is closed now," Charlie said with a bitter laugh. "There was probably no activity on his or the girls' Social Security numbers because someone has given them new names and numbers—*genuine* new identities."

"Maybe it's a mistake," I said desperately. "I'll call the agent I talked to before, and—"

"I wouldn't do that, Norma" Charlie said tiredly. "We really don't know *what* we may have tapped into here. Probably best to let sleeping dogs lie."

"What do you think it is?" I asked.

"Maybe the witness protection program. Maybe something that the general public doesn't even know exists. But it's too big for the likes of us. I'm going to tell my client that it's out of our hands. Thanks for the help, Norma."

I sat at my desk for a long time after the line went dead. There wasn't going to be a happy ending for the mother. If the mother's accusations were true, there would be no happy ending for the children either.

Finally I sighed and reached for another file folder. In my business, you learn to take the bitter with the sweet. Some things you can change and some things you can't. A smart detective soon learns to tell the difference. But it never gets any easier. Especially when you crack a case and have it snatched away by the powers that be.

19

Six Degrees of Separation—or Less

A RECENT MOVIE called *Six Degrees of Separation* explored the theme of how human beings are all connected in one way or another—and how you don't have to check any further than six individuals to find some sort of link with almost anyone in the world. I propose that you don't have to go six degrees in most cases. A true story told to me by a friend illustrates what I mean.

Back in the 1950s, an elderly man (we'll call him Uncle Harry) decided to leave the little Kentucky town where he lived and visit his nephew in Knoxville, Tennessee. So he climbed on the train for Knoxville without a word to anybody. The fly in the ointment was the fact that Uncle Harry had never been to Knoxville. In fact, Uncle Harry had never been anywhere. He had spent his entire life in an environment where everybody knew everybody else.

Even as early as 1950, some thirty years before the 1982 World's Fair opened in Knoxville, the city had a population of around 125,000. It was a fair-sized town, quite different from what Uncle Harry had been used to.

After the hour-long bus ride, the elderly man found himself standing on a busy street in front of a downtown bus station. Having absolutely no idea that things might be different in a city, he just stopped the first person he met.

"Excuse me," Uncle Harry asked, "Can you tell me where George Parker lives?"

"Is he an electrician?" the stranger inquired.

"Yes." It was one of the few things Uncle Harry knew about his nephew.

"Walk down to that corner," the man—who just happened to be an electrician belonging to the same union as George Parker—told him. "Get on the bus that says Beaumont. Tell the driver you want to get off at Barrett's Grocery. George lives in the yellow house on the corner next to the store."

Uncle Harry did as he was told. When his distraught family tracked him down and asked how he had found his nephew in a strange city where he had never traveled before, in a county that was more than five hundred square miles in size, the elderly man told them that he had simply asked directions from the first person he met. He just couldn't understand what all the fuss was about.

In my profession of finding those who have been separated from friends and family, I sometimes run across connections that are every bit as amazing.

One such case concerned a man who spent twenty years agonizing over a son born out of wedlock. The way I actually became involved with the case was just short of miraculous in itself, because of the client's reluctance to discuss what he considered to be a deep, dark secret.

My initial contact with the man began with a series of calls, which always opened with an obviously agonized request: "I need help," he would whisper. "I'm looking for my son."

As soon as I would ask for his name, the phone would go dead. For a while I couldn't decide if I was being targeted by some kind of prankster or if the calls were genuine. My mind was put at ease shortly thereafter when I received a call from a private investigator living in New York City.

My New York colleague said he had received a series of strange calls during which a man would almost sob out a request for help in finding his son. Finally the man at the other end had blurted out his problem. He lived in a medium-size town east of Nashville. But he was so ashamed by his situation that he had finally confided in an investigator several hundred miles away to decrease the risk of public humiliation.

As it turned out, his was the all-too-common story of a pregnant girlfriend whose family had pressured her to put the baby up for adoption without consulting the young father. For twenty years the man had agonized over the fate of his child. That he had fathered a son was the only information he had been given about the baby.

The New York private investigator, of course, had done the only logical thing. Flying hundreds of miles to do an investigation eats up lots of time and money. So he had contacted a local private investigator (me) whom he trusted and passed the case along.

I called the number my colleague had given me that same afternoon. I recognized the man's voice as soon as he answered.

"Mr. Tuttle?"

"Yes?"

"My name is Norma Tillman. Your case has been referred to me by one of my colleagues from New York City. I need to meet with you and discuss the matter."

"I'm sorry, but I don't know what you're talking about."

"Mr. Tuttle. I know very well that you *do* know what I'm talking about. I recognize your voice from all the times you called me for help and hung up on me. Don't you think it's about time you put this agony behind you, one way or another? I assure you that your privacy will be scrupulously protected."

Finally, after a long silence, he replied. "Yes, I think you're right. But I'd like to meet somewhere away from my office, and I don't want to come to your office either. I'm willing to drive into Nashville, though."

"All right. I do a lot of business over lunch," I told him. "Just name a time and a place and I'll be there."

≈ ≈ ≈

Michael Tuttle was a distinguished-looking man in his mid-forties. He looked a lot like the actor Kirk Douglas, only heavier. His eyes were a piercing shade of green, his jawbone angular, with a very distinctive cleft in the chin. The air of almost cocky confidence surprised me; I would never have expected such a demeanor from the man I had talked to on the phone.

"I'm glad to meet you, Mr. Tuttle—after so many false starts." I stood at the table where I had been waiting for fifteen minutes, wondering if he would actually show up, and extended my hand.

"I know it seems silly to you."

"No. It does *not* seem silly to me. Obviously it is a matter that has caused you a great deal of anguish."

"It's not just me that I'm worried about. My family is very prominent in our part of the state. I don't want to be the first member of my family to bring public embarrassment on my loved ones."

"Why don't you fill me in," I told him, "while we sit and wait for our food?"

He seemed to relax a little as the waitress took our orders, though I could tell he was scanning the room, apparently watching for familiar faces. When our drinks were on the table, he began to tell his story.

"Sharon—the girl who had my baby—was also from a prominent local family. She studied ballet and classical music. We didn't even really go steady; we were just old friends who trusted each other a lot. Do you know what I mean? Things just kind of accidentally got out of control between us."

I nodded my head neutrally, encouraging him to go on with the story.

"I wasn't in love with Sharon, but I was prepared to marry her so there wouldn't be a scandal. I guess she was wiser than I was, though—or her parents were. They sent her off, supposedly to a finishing school. She had the baby, and it was given up for adoption. I wasn't even listed as the father on the birth certificate.

"After Sharon came back and told me what had happened, we didn't ever see each other socially again, though we would run into each other from time to time. Seeing her would bring back the pain of knowing I hadn't taken care of my child.

"Not long ago, I called Sharon and asked her for whatever information she could give me about the adoption. Strangely enough, she told me everything she knew, but she made me promise not to divulge her identity if I found our son. She doesn't think her husband would be very understanding after all these years.

"So now I want to find my son," he said, a tremor in his voice. "Can you help me?"

"Give me whatever information you have, and I'll see what I can do. Let me tell you in advance, though, that I take *my* responsibilities seriously. If I find your son, he'll have to agree to see you. Otherwise, I won't pass the information on."

"That was going to be one of my conditions," he said. "I certainly don't want to cause him any problems just so I can feel better. His birthday is January 21, a little more than six months from now. If you can find him, and if he *wants* to see me, I'd like to celebrate his next birthday with him—to make up for all the ones I've missed."

≈ ≈ ≈

Some cases that look easy to begin with turn out to be impossible. Others look hard and turn out to be easy. Finding Michael Tuttle's son turned out to be of the second kind.

It just happened that I was able to bypass a lot of red tape because I had a source who was able to look into things at the agency that had handled the adoption of Michael Tuttle's infant son. Otherwise, my investigation could have been a struggle.

A few discreet calls later, I knew that Joey Freeman (his adopted name) was working in an electronics store less than twenty minutes from where I lived. It was something of a surprise to me that he had been adopted by local people, because the adoption had occurred more than two hundred miles away. But then, the whole case had been one surprising event after another.

When I walked into the electronics store and saw Joey for the first time, I didn't need documents to tell me who he was. Michael Tuttle's rakish jawbone and that remarkable cleft chin had been passed to his son. And although his eyes were blue, they had that same powerful, piercing quality.

"Can I help you?" Joey asked, obviously noticing that I had been staring at him.

"Yes, I'm looking for a voice-activated minicassette recorder."

"What will you be using it for?" he asked.

"I'm a private investigator. There are any number of uses I might put it to. I want a good-quality device."

He reached under the glass counter and laid out three different models. For the next few minutes, he reeled off details and comparisons.

In the end, I purchased a recorder, though I had not intended to. As he typed the information into his computer, preparing my receipt, he asked what I had been hoping he would ask.

"What exactly does a private investigator do?"

"Well, they do all kinds of things," I responded. "But my specialty is locating people who have been separated from loved ones or friends because of reasons beyond their control—like in divorces or adoptions."

"I'm adopted," he told me. "My parents gave me up voluntarily."

"Are you curious about your biological parents?" I asked.

"No. I always figured that people who gave up their own flesh and blood couldn't be worth all that much."

"That's not necessarily true," I said. "Sometimes there are valid reasons. And very often young fathers aren't even consulted in the matter—or maybe don't even know."

"That's all history as far as I'm concerned," Joey said, tearing off the receipt as it came out of the printer. "And I can't complain, anyway. My adoptive parents *really* wanted me. And I was also lucky enough to be adopted by people who never had to worry about money.

"I'm working here because I wanted to make it on my own," he added with a touch of cocky pride in his voice. "I could be a vice president in my father's company if I wanted to. I don't need some worthless street person showing up and trying to be a parent now."

"What if your parents turned out to be the kind of people you could admire? Would you be interested in meeting them?"

He paused for a moment and turned that movie-star face directly at me. "I think if either of my parents had been interested, they would have found me by now."

"Maybe they've been looking," I said. "Here's my card, just in case you ever change your mind."

He handed me my package, shrugged, and turned to another customer. Just for a second, though, I thought I saw a spark of longing in his eyes. And I must have been right. Two weeks later he called and made an appointment.

"Well, Joey Freemen, what can I do for you?"

He shifted uncomfortably in his chair, as if having a difficult time saying what was on his mind.

"I need to find out how much it would cost to do a search for my father."

"Why just your father?" I asked, somewhat surprised. I had feared he would also want me to find his mother, which would of course have raised another ethical dilemma.

"Well, my adoptive parents told me that my biological mother was from a good family and that she had given me up to avoid being embarrassed. I figure she could have tracked me down by now if she wanted to see me. But I got to thinking about what you said. My father may *not* have even been consulted about the matter. I thought I'd check and see if you could locate him—assuming it doesn't cost too much. I live on what I earn."

"That's an admirable trait, Joey. I'm sure your father will be glad to hear that."

"If you find him, you mean?"

"No, I don't have to find him, Joey. He's been looking for you, but he gave me orders not to let you know what was going on unless you were interested in meeting him."

"You mean my real father hired you to find me?"

"That's right, Joey. He's a phone call away."

"Where?"

"In a town not far from here. Shall I call him? He'd like to celebrate your next birthday with you."

Joey sat stunned for a moment. Then tears brimmed in his eyes. He swallowed hard and nodded his head as I reached for my telephone.

"Mr. Tuttle," I said a few moments later. "This is Norma Tillman. Would you like some company this afternoon?"

"Are you coming by with some information?" he asked hopefully.

"No. I'm sitting here with your son, Joey. I thought the two of you might want to get together today."

I held the phone and waited for the sudden sobbing at the other end to stop. Obviously a great burden had been lifted from Michael Tuttle's shoulders.

And the surprises still had not ended. There was one more in store for all of us.

~ ~ ~

"Norma, this is Michael Tuttle. Do you have time to talk for a couple of minutes?"

"Of course I do." I put aside the file I was working on and listened attentively.

"First, I wanted to let you know that Joey and I have become close. We hope his mother will eventually come around, but so far she hasn't."

"That's too bad," I said.

"Well, Joey's handling it well. He's a fine young man. There's more to the story than any of us suspected, though. I thought you might want to know."

"I love happy endings," I told him.

"Joey and I and his adopted parents have been nodding acquaintances ever since Joey was old enough to go out in public."

"How is that?" It was my turn to be startled.

"Well, I went to the University of Tennessee, and my family is full of football fans. We've always gone back to Knoxville for games, and we keep a reserved box at the football stadium. It turns out that Joey's adopted father is also a UT alumnus, and *his* family has a reserved box, too. We've been passing and nodding at each other during every home game for the last twenty years. A lot of the time, Joey was with them.

"The whole time I was worrying about my son, wondering if he had enough to eat, we were spending Saturday afternoons one stadium box apart."

"That's amazing!" I blurted. "I wonder if things would have turned out any differently if the two of you had ever stopped long enough to look each other in the face?"

"I don't know," he laughed. "We do have sort of a distinctive look, don't we?"

"Yes, Mr. Tuttle, that's for sure. Thanks for calling."

After we hung up I sat quietly for a few minutes, wondering if there was any way to compute the odds of what had happened to Michael Tuttle. Then I smiled and went back to the case I had been working on. I was glad I had been a part of bringing that biological father and son together—even though they hadn't been all that far apart.

20

Did You Think I Didn't Love You?

IN A WORK OF FICTION, the author can always end with the phrase, "They lived happily ever after." The actual wording is usually a little more sophisticated these days, but the impression is still left that everything has been worked out—once and for all— by the closing page and that nothing will ever disturb the idyllic state again.

Novelists can get away with this because a fictional story is frozen in time. The entire made-up universe revolves around the story line, and what the author says remains true forever—unless, of course, a sequel is written.

Real life, though, seldom works that way. Love affairs ebb and flow, and two people consumed by a seemingly unending passion may separate after only a few years. Maybe she will go back to school and realize that she isn't living up to her potential. Or perhaps he'll have a religious experience and take a vow of chastity. You never know. If you were being philosophical, you might say that life is a series of unending sequels, a perpetual human drama played out against the backdrop of eternity.

These thoughts came to me one afternoon as I cleaned up old files. One in particular made me freshly aware that we must grab the fleeting joys of life when we can, that we must not waste a moment of precious time.

There was more in the case jacket than one would expect to see in a private investigator's manila folders, more than dry reports and computer printouts. Frilly, feminine cards expressing a deep-felt joy and color photos of a joyous reunion between mother and daughter brought back bittersweet memories.

My initial involvement with the case was the result of a public service announcement that I ran on local television about reuniting families. Among the hundreds of replies was one that read in part:

Dear Norma,

Fifteen years ago my ex-husband took my six-year-old daughter, Candy, and I haven't seen her since. Until I saw you on television, I had no hope. If you can help find my daughter, please call me.
—Janice Dill

That letter grabbed my attention from the moment I opened it. The story it told not only offended my sense of justice and fair play, but it also touched the part of me that is a mother. I called Janice almost immediately to hear the entire story and to get enough information to begin my search.

"Janice Dill? This is Norma Tillman. You wrote a letter to me about your daughter."

For a long moment there was silence. I thought that perhaps I had the wrong number. "Is this Janice Dill?"

"Yes," she finally said, "I'm Janice. I . . . I didn't really expect to hear from you. There have been so many promises made to me through the years. And besides, I don't have a lot of money. . . ."

"Suppose I could get somebody else to pay my fees. Would you like my help in locating your daughter?"

"Why would anyone want to do that?" she asked.

"A local television station is planning a Christmas show about long-lost family members. They'll pay the bills if you'll agree to appear on the show and make an appeal to anyone who might know of your daughter's whereabouts."

"No . . ." her voice was hesitant. "I'm a very emotional person. I can't let people see me cry."

"Not even if it means you may find Candy?" I asked quietly.

"All right," she said after another long silence. "The idea scares me to death, but if it might bring my baby back, I'll do it."

"Good, Janice. Now, tell me about everything that happened up to the time of your daughter's disappearance. You never know what detail will be the one that helps me locate Candy."

"Well, it started, of course, when I married her father. He was never a nice person, but I was young and thought I was in love with him. After I got pregnant, he turned really mean."

The little tremble in her voice told me the tears were beginning. I nodded silently into the phone.

"I put up with his beatings until Candy had just turned six," she said. "By then he had gotten so violent that I was afraid for my child. I filed for divorce and moved out. He once set fire to the place where we were living—trying to scare me into going back to him."

"Did you prosecute him for arson?" I asked.

"The law said there was no proof he had done it, but I knew. He told me. When we went to court for the divorce, I begged the judge not to give him visitation rights. But he told me there was no evidence that my husband had ever been violent and that if I tried to prevent visitation I'd be in contempt of court. I was poor, and I didn't have money for a good lawyer.

"I did like I was told . . ." By now she had difficulty controlling her tears. "And the first time he . . . took her for what was . . . supposed to be a visit, I never saw her again."

"Did you report what had happened to the local police?"

"Yeah, but it didn't do no good." She sniffed, and regained a little of her composure. "The sheriff's department called it a *little domestic problem*. The report was filed away, and nobody ever did nothing about it."

"Surely the matter was reported to the FBI," I said.

"No, I don't think so. I even tried begging all my ex-husband's relatives for help. Every time I got a clue that he was someplace else, I'd call all the local schools. The man I'm married to now has paid thousands of dollars in phone bills since he married me. But done it willingly. He's a good man. I've been lucky in that.

"My ex-husband never loved our daughter," she said bitterly. "He just took her for spite. It's been fifteen years, and not a word. Every time I see a little blond girl, I think of Candy, even though I know she's grown." Now Janice began to sob. I waited, giving her time to recover.

"Janice, if your daughter can be found, I intend to do it. I want you to give me every scrap of information you have on Candy, from nicknames and scars to her Social Security number, if you have it. Also, I'll need the most current picture you can find."

Three days later, I sat in my office with the newly opened file in front of me. I had calmed down a little, had put aside the rage and indignation that had grown in me as I listened to Janice tell her sad tale.

Things have improved a little in recent years. Law enforcement officers, for the most part, have finally come to view parental kidnapping as a *real* crime, not just a domestic dispute. But it's still possible for such cases to fall through the cracks. Even the most well-intentioned law officer can do only so much in such cases.

But *I* can do more. I have made it my job, my passion, and my profession to help people like Janice. I sat and looked at the picture of Candy Dill, the last one her mother had made. The little girl with curly hair and blue eyes was sitting on Santa's lap. I sincerely hoped her mother would see her again before another Christmas passed. But if that was to happen, I had to get to work.

First, on the outside chance that Candy's father had not changed her name, I tapped into my database of proper names.

As I expected, there was no information on Candy Dill. Happily, however, I struck gold with my next database. The computer located a young woman in Oregon who was using Candy Dill's Social Security number. The birthdate was also a match.

There was no phone listing for the young woman in the town where she had last noted her Social Security number on a rental application, but that was not an insurmountable problem. I linked up with another database to which I subscribe, and within minutes I had telephone numbers for almost everyone else on the block.

I contacted several people on the list and asked them to have Candy (or Patricia Clark as she was known there) to call me. I waited expectantly for that call for several days, then phoned more of her neighbors and left the same message with them. It seemed impossible that someone had not informed her that I was trying to reach her.

My deadline for the television show was rapidly approaching. It began to appear that I would have to use another family for the reunion. It saddened me to think that the mother and daughter would miss this opportunity to be reunited. I was just about to give up when my phone rang one night. The voice at the other end was terse and to the point. There was no warmth in it.

"Everywhere I go, people keep telling me that you're trying to find me. I'd like to know why."

"Is this Patricia Clark?" I asked.

"Yes."

"Is your real name Candy Dill?"

"Who wants to know?"

"Your mother."

"How do I know you're not working for my father?"

"So, you're hiding from *him* under an assumed name?"

"I've had a lot of names. He jerked me around the country until I was able to get away from him, and he gave me a different name every time we stopped somewhere. I escaped from him while he was in jail, and I don't intend for him to ever hurt me again."

"You'll just have to take a chance, Candy. I'm sitting here looking at a picture your mother gave me. You're on Santa's lap. Do you remember that picture?"

"No. I can't remember anything before we started moving around. He always told me that my mother didn't want me. I used to dream that she really loved me, but it was just a fantasy." Her voice had lost its hard edge.

"It wasn't a fantasy, Candy," I said. "Your mother has always loved you. She's spent the last fifteen years searching for you—and she didn't get a lot of help from the authorities."

The voice on the phone had now taken on a little-girl breathlessness. "You're saying my mother is really trying to find me? She really does love me?"

"Yes, Candy. Yes to both questions! And if you're interested, I can reunite the two of you before Christmas, and somebody else will pay all your expenses."

"All right." She was suddenly crying and her cries sounded for all the world like a whimpering puppy.

"Candy," I said softly, "your life is about to get better."

"It already has," she whispered. "It already has."

A few days later, Janice Dill, her second husband, and their daughter made their appearance on a local television variety show. It wasn't easy for Janice. A very emotional and private person, she did her best to stay in control.

Thinking she was one of several guests who would tell their stories and make an appeal for help, Janice shredded several tissues as she talked. When she had finished, the television host said, "I hope your holidays will be better from now on."

"I wish they would," Janice said, tears glistening in her eyes.

"Well, today *is* your day," the host said. "Norma has located your daughter, and here she is!"

A freight train of emotions passed over Janice Dill's face as Candy walked across the stage. A dainty, pale young woman, Candy seemed almost in a trance.

"She's so pretty," Janice whispered an instant before she

rushed to embrace the daughter she hadn't seen in fifteen years. Then, as they clung to each other, Janice asked, "Honey, did you think I didn't love you?"

"I didn't know what to think," Candy replied truthfully.

The show went on for several more minutes, but it was obvious that everyone else had ceased to exist for the mother and daughter. The rest of us were mere spectators at a reunion of body and soul and heart and spirit.

I'm not much of a weeper, but we all wiped away tears that day. You couldn't watch that kind of naked emotion and remain unaffected.

There are some who find lost loved ones and then allow petty problems to drive wedges between them. Such was not the case with Candy and Janice. They made up for lost time.

As each new phase in their lives opened, I would receive a card or letter from Candy, always done in her dainty cursive hand, thanking me for what I had done. I was repaid many times over for my work in that case.

Within months of the reunion, I flew to Oregon to participate in Candy's wedding. When she told me that it was as if I had become a second mother to her, I was deeply moved. But I told her no mother could love her with more faithfulness and courage than her own mother had.

No sooner had I gotten used to the idea of the little blond girl all grown up and married than news came that she was expecting a baby. And Janice was there to enjoy every minute of it. When Candy called to tell me about her pregnancy, I felt almost as if I had another grandchild of my own on the way.

I meant to check on her more often than I did, but I was busy. You know how it is, don't you? Sometimes you fall behind on important things.

The call that came in before daybreak one morning started with joy and ended with a fresh understanding of just how fragile human existence can be, a new reason to hold nothing back.

"Candy had a little girl," Janice said in a choked voice.

"That's wonderful," I began, noticing for the first time the early hour on the digital clock by my bed. I realized that Janice would not have called at such an hour just to announce a birth.

A sense of dread gripped me in its icy talons. "Is something wrong, Janice?"

"The baby is fine." I heard a catch in her voice. "But Candy died. It was internal bleeding. Nobody noticed until it was too late."

I was too stunned to reply. There was silence on the line for perhaps a full minute. I wanted to comfort Janice, but I couldn't. I didn't know what to say.

"I know she would have wanted me to call you right away. Candy felt that we owed you for the time we had together—even though, as things turned out, it wasn't very long."

"Will you let me know . . . ?"

"I'll call you as soon as arrangements are made. God bless you, Norma."

I managed to choke out "You too, Janice," just before the line went silent.

For a while, I couldn't think about Candy without tearing up. Poor little thing. It seemed such a cruel trick of fate that a daughter lost for fifteen years, then found, should have been snatched away so quickly.

After a while, though, when the pain had subsided somewhat, I realized that a short period of joy can ease an awful lot of suffering. We humans have such a short visit on Earth, not even enough time to get used to being here, really.

God takes the long view, though. And He doesn't make any mistakes. And I thank God from the bottom of my heart that I am allowed to have a hand in bringing people together. As I've said before, I'm in this work for the happy endings. But happy endings or not, I believe that all will be well.

For information about Norma Tillman's
services and products, send a self-addressed,
stamped envelope to:

Norma Tillman
Dept. 995
P.O. Box 290333
Nashville, TN 37229-0333

Internet address: http://www.reunion.com/reunion

E-mail: norma@reunion.com